I0455859

Editor-in-Chief and Founder:
  Lyndon H. LaRouche, Jr.
Editorial Board: *Lyndon H. LaRouche, Jr. , Helga
  Zepp-LaRouche, Robert Ingraham, Tony
  Papert, Gerald Rose, Dennis Small, Jeffrey
  Steinberg, William Wertz*
Co-Editors: *Robert Ingraham, Tony Papert*
Managing Editor: *Nancy Spannaus*
Technology: *Marsha Freeman*
Books: *Katherine Notley*
Ebooks: *Richard Burden*
Graphics: *Alan Yue*
Photos: *Stuart Lewis*
Circulation Manager: *Stanley Ezrol*

INTELLIGENCE DIRECTORS
Counterintelligence: *Jeffrey Steinberg, Michele
  Steinberg*
Economics: *John Hoefle, Marcia Merry Baker,
  Paul Gallagher*
History: *Anton Chaitkin*
Ibero-America: *Dennis Small*
Russia and Eastern Europe: *Rachel Douglas*
United States: *Debra Freeman*

INTERNATIONAL BUREAUS
Bogotá: *Miriam Redondo*
Berlin: *Rainer Apel*
Copenhagen: *Tom Gillesberg*
Houston: *Harley Schlanger*
Lima: *Sara Madueño*
Melbourne: *Robert Barwick*
Mexico City: *Gerardo Castilleja Chávez*
New Delhi: *Ramtanu Maitra*
Paris: *Christine Bierre*
Stockholm: *Ulf Sandmark*
United Nations, N.Y.C.: *Leni Rubinstein*
Washington, D.C.: *William Jones*
Wiesbaden: *Göran Haglund*

ON THE WEB
e-mail: eirns@larouchepub.com
www.larouchepub.com
www.executiveintelligencereview.com
www.larouchepub.com/eiw
Webmaster: *John Sigerson*
Assistant Webmaster: *George Hollis*
Editor, Arabic-language edition: *Hussein Askary*

EIR (ISSN 0273-6314) *is published weekly
(50 issues), by EIR News Service, Inc.,
P.O. Box 17390, Washington, D.C. 20041-0390.
(703) 777-9451*

European Headquarters: E.I.R. GmbH, Postfach
Bahnstrasse 9a, D-65205, Wiesbaden, Germany
Tel: 49-611-73650
Homepage: http://www.eirna.com
e-mail: eirna@eirna.com
Director: Georg Neudecker

Montreal, Canada: 514-461-1557

Denmark: EIR - Danmark, Sankt Knuds Vej 11,
basement left, DK-1903 Frederiksberg, Denmark.
Tel.: +45 35 43 60 40, Fax: +45 35 43 87 57. e-mail:
eirdk@hotmail.com.

Mexico City: EIR, Sor Juana Inés de la Cruz 242-2
Col. Agricultura C.P. 11360
Delegación M. Hidalgo, México D.F.
Tel. (5525) 5318-2301
eirmexico@gmail.com

Canada Post Publication Sales Agreement
#40683579

Postmaster: Send all address changes to *EIR*, P.O.
Box 17390, Washington, D.C. 20041-0390.

Signed articles in *EIR* represent the views of the
authors, and not necessarily those of the Editorial
Board.

Our Mission
To Mortality

EIR Contents

www.larouchepub.com Volume 43, Number 28, July 8, 2016

Cover This Week

Left to right: Bass-baritone William Warfield (1920-2002), baritone Dorceal Duckens, and longtime Lyndon LaRouche associate Dennis Speed, gathered around Sylvia Olden Lee (1917-2004), at a 1991 Schiller Institute conference.

EIRNS/Stuart Lewis

I. Berlin Schiller Institute Conference

A Common Future for Mankind and A Renaissance of Classical Culture

EIR's July 1 issue provided extensive coverage of the Schiller Institute's international conference held in Berlin, Germany, June 25-26, 2016. The full texts of four addresses summarized in the July 1 *EIR* are presented here. All were given on June 25. They are the addresses of Col. Alain Corvez (France) and Col. Ulrich Scholz (Germany) from Panel I, and Marco Zanni (Italy) and Daisuke Kotegawa (Japan) from Panel II.

ALAIN CORVEZ

Will American Hubris End by Choice, Or in a Universal Combustion?

Col. (ret.) Alain Corvez is an international consultant and a former adviser to the French defense and interior ministries. He titled his address, "Will the American Hubris Come to an End, or Will It Disappear with Us in a Universal Combustion?"

I would like to congratulate the Schiller Institute for organizing this conference at a critical moment, when the threat of a nuclear war—which would lead to the extinction of humanity—becomes clearer by the day, because of the concentration in the heart of Europe of weapons capable of destroying the planet within seconds. To respond to the reinforcement of U.S. strategic forces in NATO on European territory, Russia has had to deploy an equivalent arsenal of deterrence on its western borders. It is high time that the strategists of various countries, even those far from the European theater, demand restraint and more wisdom from the heads of state of the entire world. That is the purpose of this beneficial initiative by Mrs. Helga Zepp-La-Rouche, whom I wish to compliment personally.

And as we are immersed in the humanist thinking of Schiller, I would like to recall how Nietzsche described him in his introduction to *On the Future of our Educational Institutions*.

Between those who take everything for granted and those who are solitary [out of despair], there stand the *fighters*—that is to say, those who still have hope, and as the noblest and sublimest example of this class, we recognize Schiller as he is described by Goethe in his *Epilogue to Schiller's 'Song of the Bell'*:

Brighter now glow'd his cheek, and still
    more bright.
With that unchanging, ever-youthful glow,—
That courage which overcomes, in hard-
    fought fight,
Sooner or later, ev'ry earthly foe—
That faith which, soaring to the realms of
    light,
Now boldly presseth on, now bendeth low,
So that the good may work, wax, thrive
    amain,
So that the day the noble may attain.

In his first work, *Philosophy During the Tragic Age of the Greeks*, Nietzsche writes of Heraclitus:

… he believes in an end of the world periodically repeating itself, and in an ever-renewed emerging of another world out of the all-destroying world-fire. The period during which the world hastens towards that world-fire and the dissolution into pure fire is characterized by him most strikingly as a *demand* and a *need;* the state of being completely swallowed up by the fire as satiety.…

He continues, "satiety gives birth to crime: Hubris."

Indeed, the overabundance of means, excess, the immeasurable pride that define hubris are crimes against humanity, a humanity that needs caution and measure. For Nietzsche, Heraclitus was the "weeping philosopher," as he was called in later antiquity:

Is not the whole world-process now an act of punishment of the Hubris?… Is not the guilt now shifted into the essence of the things and indeed, the world of Becoming and of individuals accordingly exonerated from guilt; yet at the same time are they not condemned forever and ever to bear the consequences of guilt?

We know that Heraclitus later believed that everything that tends to be contradictory converges into harmony, which is invisible for the common man, and that what is to become is the result of the struggle among opposites, which affords us some hope that justice will prevail over injustice.

That is far from the nihilist vision of Schopenhauer: "We expiate our birth once by our life and a second time by our death."

The Atomic Weapon: For War or Peace?

Our world is one which has seen the accumulation of gigantic means of destruction since the appearance of the nuclear weapon in our arsenals. It is a deadly weapon which, as General de Gaulle said, was not a step in a simple progression in weapons technology, but a technological leap, upsetting the traditional rules of warfare as—for the first time in the history of mankind—man invented a weapon which it were impossible to use, once more than one country possessed it. Exclusively a deterrent weapon, and thus the assurance for any country that has it, that no hostile power would take the risk of being destroyed at the moment that it attacked. But impossible to use reasonably, hence the name, "weapon of non-use."

In the field of science, de Gaulle thought that the electron microscope represented a similar leap:

I do not believe, you see, that the electron microscope is only an enormous pair of glasses: What it allows us to discover, is not what we were looking for. It solves some of our problems, but it also brings its own. We have not finished with the atomic bomb. The most powerful means of war began by bringing peace. A strange peace, but nonetheless peace. Let us wait and see.

The great, recently deceased French anthropologist and philosopher, René Girard, who invented the mimetic theory, wrote in *The Unknown Voice of the Real*, in reference to Nietzsche:

True vengeance [in the sense of Nietzschean *ressentiment* —ed.] is again with us in the form of the absolute nuclear weapon, which reduces our planet to the size of a primitive village, once again terrified by the prospect of a war to the death. True vengeance is so terrifying that its staunchest supporters dare not release it, since they know full well that all the atrocities they can inflict on their enemies, can also be inflicted on them by those enemies.[1]

1. René Girard, "Nietzsche Against the Crucified One," in his *La voix méconnue du réel: Une théorie des mythes archaïques et modernes.* Paris: Grasset, 2002.

What doctrine would Heraclitus have formulated, had he known of the potential for mankind to unleash nuclear fusion, when he had already spoken of a "world-fire"?

One great French strategist, General Pierre-Marie Gallois, who honored me by bringing me into his think tank, told me of his exchanges with General de Gaulle on the nuclear weapon, and how so few people, even among specialists, had understood the new concept. They continued to think in terms of military coercion, whereas it was all about deterring an attack on us.

I quote him:

Suddenly plunged into the atomic era, opinion continued to reason as it could have rationally continued to do in the classical cycle. Everyone thought in terms of coercion, when deterrence was at stake. They compared the forces available numerically, when they should have assessed the damage that the strongest would suffer, no matter how powerful, if it attacked the weakest.[2]

Role Reversal

Right now NATO is engaged in an unheard of classical and nuclear military build-up in Europe, in particular on Russia's borders, in Poland, and in the Baltic States, in addition to the forces already stationed in Romania, Italy, Germany, and Poland. I will not go into the details of the forces deployed, which have already been described with great precision by many experts. Those forces of the Atlantic Organization include nuclear forces as part of the global AEGIS system that the United States had originally announced was aimed at countering the threat from Iran, although it was clear to everyone that the purpose was to threaten a re-emerging Russia. This system, which is also deployed in the Atlantic and the Pacific, has sea-, air-, and land-based mobile installations. Although presented as defensive against a hypothetical Russian or Chinese threat, it is in fact also offensive, and its cruise or ballistic missiles can be used in a first strike.

France, which unfortunately returned to NATO military organization during the Sarkozy presidency, is involved in this war-like deployment and just recently decided to allow NATO forces to be stationed on her territory, although in principle only those belonging to the military staffs in which our senior and noncommissioned officers have now become used to carrying out brilliant careers, and who are therefore not inclined to see NATO as a U.S. military tool, but rather as an alliance of the free and righteous world that defends liberalism and human rights against another world which is not.

AEGIS is a worldwide system capable of launching a nuclear attack anywhere on the planet. It is presented to public opinion with the lie that it is defensive, but its purpose is to convey to the world that the United States is the master of the planet and intends to tell every country how to live, what rules to follow, which customs to keep and which to discard, carrying out completely free trade by eliminating protective tariffs and maybe even borders. The United States intends to impose its model at the risk of triggering a nuclear war that would be the Apocalypse, or the final conflagration that Heraclitus spoke of in the Sixth Century B.C. The European Union has cast in stone—in the stone of its founding treaties—this rule of unbridled liberalism, of free and undistorted trade, of elimination of internal borders, just as it has structurally integrated its defense into the military organization of NATO.

The entire U.S. military system—with its unmatched budget of more than $700 billion, when all the funds of defense and intelligence organizations are combined—is now directed against China and Russia, because of their alleged hegemonic ambitions in Europe for one, in Asia for the other, thereby reversing the roles.[3] This strategy draws in its allies, especially the EU—of which France is the acolyte—but it certainly seems doomed to implosion with the help of our British friends, who seem to want to get off the ship before the shipwreck. (As I write, we do not yet know the results of the June 23 referendum on the proposed British exit from the EU, but whatever the outcome, it will have an enormous impact on the future of the EU and should hasten its break-up.)

China Emerges with Win-Win Approach

China, through its laborious and industrious efforts, has made tremendous economic progress, eradicating famine and underdevelopment for a majority of the population. It has created a large wealthy class,

---

2. Intervention of General Gallois in a colloquium organized in September 1984 at Arc-et-Senans by the Institut Charles de Gaulle and the Université de Franche-Comté.

3. The largest defense budgets in the 2015 worldwide survey of the International Institute for Strategic Studies were $597.5 billion for the United States, $145.8 billion for China, $81.9 billion for Saudi Arabia, $65.5 billion for Russia, $56.2 billion for the UK, $48 billion for India, and $46.8 billion for France, which comes in seventh.

raised the overall living standard, and accumulated significant financial reserves. At the same time, it maintains the centralism of collectivist communism, which gives it the great advantage of maintaining central control over opening its immense population to world trade and control over the major adaptive reforms. The opposite happened in the Soviet Union, which quickly dissolved under the *perestroika* of a Gorbachov who had good intentions, but lost control of the reform process.

China is considered a rival by the United States, to be destroyed before it gets too powerful. Therefore, it is denied the right to defend its vital interests, in particular in the surrounding seas, by creating hostile alliances of those countries that value U.S. protection.

But in fact, China's fine-tuned diplomacy has convinced a growing number of countries in the region that China is not imperial, and rather wishes to favor international cooperation—to develop economic projects that are profitable for all. The immense projects in the program proposed to Eurasian countries, but also open to the rest of the world, called the New Silk Road and Belt, have already convinced many countries. These countries have joined in institutions that come up with such projects and finance them, such as the Asian Infrastructure Investment Bank (AIIB) and the Shanghai Cooperation Organization (SCO), the BRICS, and ASEAN, which is joined by Iran, at the crossroads of the Middle East and Caucasian Asia, with the 400 million inhabitants in the immediate vicinity. Also, the Bolivarian Alliance for America (ALBA) and the Union of South American Nations (UNASUR) in Latin America.

Certain countries continue to play both ways, remaining friendly with America while trading with China and Russia, but the impression is that their economic and even strategic interests draw them closer to the win-win system, which has seen previously rival parties put aside their demands to become part of this new world order. India and China are one example of that, but not the only one.

Russia Faces U.S. Imperial Hysteria

U.S. diplomacy presents Russia as an imperial power ready to invade Europe. But that is such a blatant falsehood that one wonders how European countries can accept the idea, unless they have some reason to link up with the United States to avoid having to spend more on their own defense. This falsehood seems to have recently lost ground in Brussels, where, under the pressure of different peoples and countries, it is recognized that the sanctions are more harmful for EU member states than for Russia, which is developing options in Asia and on its own immense territory.

On June 8, the French Senate voted up a proposal to gradually lift the sanctions, after the National Assembly had done so in April. And the President of the EU, Jean-Claude Juncker, attended the St. Petersburg International Economic Forum this month, as he could no longer resist the pressure coming from deep within the real Europe, which has no problem understanding that entente and cooperation with the immense country of Russia is required for its future.

This, of course, is worrisome for Washington, which has viewed Western Europe as a protective barrier against Soviet Russia since 1945. After its victory over Soviet communism in 1989 and the dissolution of the USSR, a certain hubris or overconfidence inspired America to destroy the new Russia by buying up politicians and oligarchs and supporting Chechen terrorism in various ways. Putin, an astute strategist who understands the workings of the balance of power, wished to put an end to his country's disintegration. He wished to come to an understanding with the number-one power in the world, accepting the concessions imposed by its weakness, but less and less inclined to sacrifice the vital interests of Russia, vital interests that were threatened by the U.S. imperial hysteria, which presented the one attacked as the attacker.

Frankly speaking, what serious strategist could imagine that Russian divisions would invade Eastern Europe to reconquer the former satellites of the Soviet Union? What for? To what purpose? To grab their mineral or industrial wealth, or to convert them to the Orthodox faith?

All experts know that the purpose of stopping the coup in Georgia in August 2008, was to clearly demonstrate what the limits were of NATO's constant eastward expansion, in violation of the promises made, after the U.S. State Department-led provocations by the Tiblisi government. The return of Crimea to its fatherland in 2014, after a unanimous vote of the population, was a result of the "open coup d'état"—described as such by the American strategist George Friedman—which had brought to power in Kiev a government hostile to the populations in the Ukrainian East and to Moscow. The vote was compliant with the UN rules on the right of peoples to self determination.

Wake Up from Your Messianic Dream

Putin's reemerging Russia attempted for a long time to come to an agreement with the United States and its European neighbors, but the hegemonic intentions of part of the oligarchy in Washington could not accept that the world could be multipolar, and that America could share the running of the planet with new powers. Apparently, the presidential candidate Donald Trump hopes to break this shortsighted system. We can hope he will succeed in breaking this system, for the sake of the world and of the Americans, since he proposes to put an end to military interventionism, to cooperate with Russia and talk to China, in order to focus on development of the national economy by bringing back the pension funds that have gone abroad for more profit, and to invest them in the U.S. economy to create jobs. That is why he is caricatured in Western media as a clown, although American citizens have understood his message and vote for him.

It is misleading to accuse Russia of massing military forces on the borders of Poland and the Baltic states with aggressive intentions, since Moscow built up its forces there in response to NATO's repeated threats at its doorstep, especially in the Baltic countries. Former U.S. Secretary of Defense Chuck Hagel recently stated that NATO's build-up near Russia was a mistake and counterproductive.

That is why I spoke of the hubris or hysteria of the United States, because it does not seem to realize that this military escalation against Russia raises extreme fear in the entire world, because it involves nuclear weapons. It is obvious that Russia will not accept to be crushed without attacking at the same level. That would not mean World War III but the end of humanity.

It is time for the most important world power, at least militarily—in terms of its arsenals and the number of bases around the world—to become measured and to cease refusing to see the world that is changing, the balances that are shifting, the emergent powers that are asserting themselves. It is time for that power to decide to enter into cooperation for the benefit of all, with the most powerful assisting the poorest, and scientific progress serving all of humanity.

The United States' excessiveness and blindness are the result of a messianic conception, a conception that brought to power politicians who are convinced—ever since the collapse of communism in the USSR—that since the supreme good (liberalism) defeated the absolute evil (totalitarian collectivism), the United States is entrusted with the divine mission of leading the world. That is the origin of the drama of our time.

In addition, there are the interests of the financial powers organized in lobbies in Washington, whose assets cover a large part of the planet and who own the media and their means of propaganda. These networks are the actual decision makers of U.S. policy, so much so that the government is often unable to implement its own decisions if they are not acceptable to those interests. In that respect, the Obama Administration did manage to impose a few reforms, such as medical insurance domestically and the nuclear deal with Iran, but the financial powers and their interests are still there.

This Confrontation Cannot Succeed

Now nearing the end of his term, the U.S. President appears to have given in to the demands of the financial powers, in particular in Syria where, despite the announcements of agreements with Russia to end the bloodbath, the actions on the ground continue to fuel the fighting. Taken off guard by the Russian military intervention in September 2015, which forced the players to take off their masks and choose between fighting Islamic terrorism or not, the U.S. leaders have continued the policy of regime change against any government that does not accept their policy, which greatly benefits an Israel which uses the chance to deny more rights of Palestinians and take their territory, in total violation of UN rules.

Russia, with its intervention in Syria, demonstrated that it has developed an army whose technology is on a par with that of the United States, and is even more modern in certain areas. Though the Russian army is not as large and does not have foreign bases, which proves it has no imperial agenda, it is capable of coping with any deliberate attack on its vital interests. Russia has shown that it hopes to cooperate with the United States, the Europeans, China, India, and Asia more generally. The confrontationist stance maintained by the U.S. government—which refuses to acknowledge that its worldwide supremacy is over, but that it could cooperate peacefully with other countries rather than encouraging tensions and wars as it has done since 2001—cannot succeed against the plans of the rest of the world.

The refusal of the United States to recognize the new realities, the desire to sustain an outmoded order—illustrated by a paper money that finances its debt but not its development—threatens to end the world in a nuclear Apocalypse. All the countries in which the United States has intervened, from Afghanistan to

Libya, have been destroyed, while the Middle East is in dramatic chaos. The United States' policy in Syria is ambiguous, as it plays several cards at the same time, simultaneously supporting rival forces, agreeing with Russia one day and rejecting a possible solution the next, and endorsing the religious antagonisms constantly fanned by Saudi Arabia.

These contradictions are also visible in U.S. policy toward Iran, a major, indispensable actor of stability in the Middle East and the Caucasus. The United States signed the agreement reintegrating Iran into the concert of nations, but continually threatens to ostracize it again, and even threatens to take financial reprisals against countries that interact with Tehran too quickly.

New Warsaw Pact

We know today that NATO will be holding a summit in Warsaw in early July, following on the major Anakonda maneuvers under U.S. aegis, with the participation of 24 countries—including Macedonia and Albania (!), and of course the Baltic countries, Turkey, Canada, and Finland—but fortunately without France. This is symbolic, since the Warsaw Pact ceased to exist after the dissolution of the USSR and what we hoped was the end of the Cold War. Such a summit, in such a place, sounds like a useless and dangerous challenge, especially given the reinforcement of NATO's nuclear weapons in Europe.

Russia is not a threat to anyone. It is simply organizing economic and strategic cooperation with the Asians, and with Africa and Latin America. It would be willing to do so with the United States and Europe, but the latter is still too subservient to Washington to take up the offer, although some attempts can be detected to shake off the chains of servitude, due to popular pressure.

That is why, as a French patriot, I would like France to withdraw from NATO and refuse to take part in the Warsaw summit, the purpose of which is to provoke Russia. I am described on various websites, in articles, and in books as being pro-Russian, or pro-Chinese, pro-Iranian, or rabidly anti-American. In fact, I am simply pro-French and convinced that my country's interest is to see the world as it is, to shake off any "bloc" ideology, and to respect the sovereignty of states. I would like to see France recover its own sovereignty, and to resume the independent policy which was her tradition from the time of General de Gaulle, which does not rule out agreements with our neighbors.

Our era is experiencing the return of national sentiment in Europe, as the impression sets in that, to avoid disappearing into a shapeless hodgepodge, the various peoples need to defend their heritage and enrich it through exchanges with the others. A Europe of the nations is called upon to replace the technocratic EU, which is unable to meet the great challenges of our time. Its sincere acolytes are beginning to understand that, to build it, "it is not enough to jump up and down on one's chair like a little goat, bleating Europe, Europe, Europe" [as de Gaulle once said], and that that doesn't help at all.

I don't believe Robert F. Kennedy, Jr., could be considered anti-American or a traitor. However, he does judge the policy of his country the same way I do, in a article in *Politico* of February 24, 2016 entitled, "Why the Arabs don't want us in Syria." He wrote, "They don't hate 'our freedoms.' They hate that we've betrayed our ideals in their own countries—for oil." He adds the Iranians to his catalogue, recalling the overthrow of Mossadegh in 1953 by the CIA, after the British MI6 had failed to do so.

Conclusion

It is high time for American hubris to be replaced by a spirit of cooperation, which the entire world would greet with relief—a cooperation among all countries on the basis of mutual respect and shared interests. In such a calmed climate among nations, gradual but total nuclear disarmament should be on the agenda, and the nuclear powers should agree to proceed with it simultaneously. France, which has proved its greatness in the past in defending universal values, could contribute to this process when the other nations concerned have renounced their threats. But deterrence, which has so far prevented a new, deadly world war, will have to continue in one way or another to guarantee planetary peace.

To conclude, I would like to quote a great French philosopher who was also an extraordinary statesman, General de Gaulle. In a 1964 address to students at the University of Mexico, he said:

Indeed, beyond the distances that are shrinking, beyond the ideologies that are weakening, and the political systems that are losing their breath, and *unless humanity destroys itself some day in a monstrous self-destruction*, the fact that will dominate the future is the unity of our universe: One cause, that of man; one necessity, that of world progress, and consequently of assistance to all those countries that desire it in order to develop; one duty, that of peace; these constitute for our species, the very basis of existence.

ULRICH SCHOLZ

The Pathology of the Western Paradigm of Warfare

Lt. Col. (ret.) Ulrich Scholz of Germany is a former fighter pilot, NATO planner, and lecturer on air warfare.

Schön guten Morgen! Good morning! I'm going to talk to you about war, and I am going to call it a pathology of the West.

Let me start first by saying a few words about myself, so that you get the feeling that I'm not just a naïve peace activist. I have been a warrior half of my life: I'm an American-trained fighter pilot; I knew how to drop bombs. I taught people how to drop bombs, even nuclear bombs, and I enjoyed it. I got my General Staff education with the U.S. Air Force. I'm very fond of American culture. I have a lot of American friends, very good people. And I think I have to say that, because what I am going to say next might cause you to doubt that I am still very friendly with America.

I am going to use three metaphors, and I'm going to teach you three questions to ask, to come to the conclusion that war must not no longer be a means of politics. So that's the bottom line. I use metaphors because I have learned that it is the best way to get adults to learn without them knowing that they're learning.

Two metaphors on this picture: Who knows the movie from which this picture comes? Say it louder,— "Planet of the Apes," that's right. And I am not going to tell you the plot of the movie, because the movie fits right into the center of what this conference is all about. At the break, if some of you don't know, I will tell you. It's worth watching, with Charlton Heston; and if you haven't seen it yet, just get the DVD; it's fascinating.

Clausewitz on War

OK. It all started with these two sympathetic people, Carl von Clausewitz, a young general of the Prussian army, and his wife. [**Slide 1**] After the Napoleonic wars, Clausewitz sat down and tried to grasp the essentials of war by studying Napoleon, and he wrote the book, *On War*. Unfortunately, he died before he could finish it. So his wife Marie finished the book after the first chapter. She took his notes and wrote the book. It was an extraordinary thing for a woman at that time to write a book on war.

One of Clausewitz's essentials is the famous dictum: "War is the continuation of politics by other means." Again, it is a reduction of a description of what he stud-

SLIDE 1

War is merely the continuation of politics by other means.

On War

Carl von Clausewitz
1780 - 1831

Marie von Clausewitz
1779-1836

War must not be a means of politics anymore.

150 Million casualties

4000 Nuclear Weapons

International Law

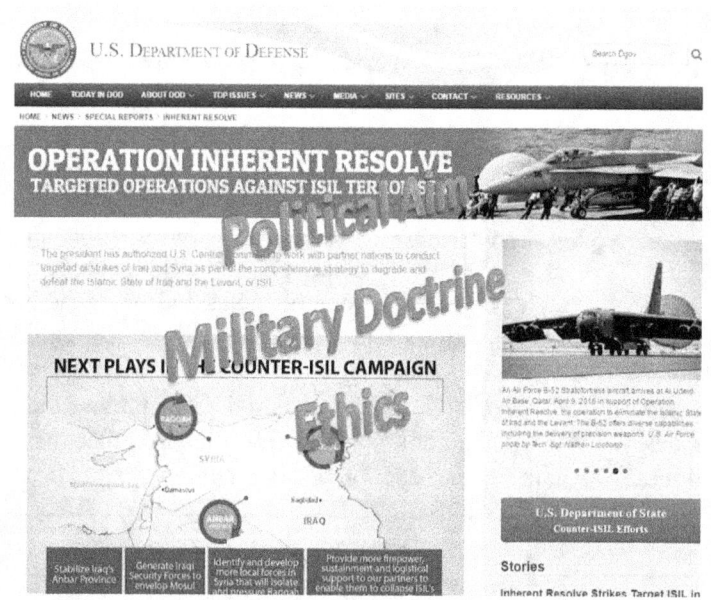

ied. And now the unbelievable: Politicians and generals still, today, take this, Clausewitz's observation, like a cookbook. We must just study wars to apply it properly, to drive home political interests. And this is a scandal. If you look at the facts, in the last 200 years, in major wars, we have had more than 150 million dead. At the moment, we have 4,000 nuclear weapons, armed, active, in this world. And in our charters of international law, we have it written that war is prohibited. [**Slide 2**]

But politicians and generals still think about how to use war to drive home interests. I think there is some

pathology behind that. Because, with these facts, I think nobody who is sensitive,— I always say, "War is an offense to human intelligence." Because if you look at these facts, who could think of going to war? [applause] Thank you.

I am going to use a little rhyme that Goethe, the famous German poet, used as a metaphor. He wrote,

In breathing, there are two graces,
Drawing the air in, and exhaling it.
One constrains, and the other refreshes.
So wondrously life is mixed.
You thank God when He presses you,
And thank him when He once again
releases you.

Now, I am comparing this metaphor of breathing to the capitalist system. For me, breathing in, is growth. In our systems we have learned to inhale; unfortunately, we have forgotten how to exhale. And war is for me, the ultimate, desperate way to try to inhale. You know, the disease behind this is asthma; people with asthma people cannot exhale. The Western economic system is asthmatic.

So what do we have to do, to get a balanced way of breathing into our world? A change of paradigm, that's what we talk about. We must change. And my first step to that is to let go of this old war paradigm. That is where I want to get to.

The Three Questions

Now to the three questions. If you read or hear about a government going to war, you should always put it into question, and ask questions about these three things: What is the political aim? How does the military propose to achieve it? And what about our ethics when we do it? These three questions you can address to all wars throughout history, and I have just looked at the last 25 years of wars the West has waged. The West *fails* in all three. And still, it goes to war.

I am going to use the current Operation Inherent Resolve. That is the American bombing campaign against Daesh, the Islamic State, just to show you how these three things are flawed.

The Pentagon's homepage for Operation Inherent

Resolve is http://www.inherentresolve.mil. It is accessible to the public. [**Slide 3**] One thing a political aim must always have, for the military to go after it with military means, is an end-state. If the military has done its job, what does the world look like? And as we are in the West, and we like controlling, we like *numbers*. We like to have a figure. And on this homepage, you can find it: Every day they update the targets they have hit and destroyed. You can see it every day. Here it is for May 31, 2016.

They started counting in 2014. Unfortunately, they haven't given a number that, when reached, means that we have won. So you can do this counting forever. In Vietnam, they lost over counting —"body count." You know that. They're doing it again. [applause] That's pathological, isn't it?

If you read, "destroyed buildings, 6,500," I ask myself, "who else was in the building besides terrorists? Who was in the neighboring building?"

So political aims must be clearly defined. There must be a clear statement of what the military must do. I will give you the political aims of Inherent Resolve. The first is "to militarily defeat Daesh, to increase regional stability." Is there any stability in this region? Is there anything we can increase? Read it! It's official. "To increase regional stability." That's fooling themselves, and fooling us. This is baloney.

A second political aim is "to defeat the ideology of Daesh." How can you defeat an ideology by dropping bombs? Tell me! "To stem the global flow of foreign fighters in all of our nations." Bombing in the Middle East will "stem the flow of terrorists in all of our nations." Can you do this militarily? [**Slides 4, 5**]

So these two political aims are the basis of all the bombing we do there every day. You could stop right there. What a waste of lives and money!

Next, military doctrine. President Obama said, in September 2014, that no U.S. ground forces will be used to fight Daesh. Doctrine is the *way* we fight. And after Vietnam, the United States developed a doctrine of jointness: We use everything we have in our stock—Army, Navy, Air Force, Special Forces. We look at the problem and then we decide, can we do it, and how do we want to do it. Obama said, "no ground

SLIDE 4

SLIDE 5

OPERATION INHERENT RESOLVE
TARGETS DAMAGED/DESTROYED*

Tanks	143
HMMWVs	382
Staging Areas	1,627
Buildings	6,545
Fighting Positions	7,824
Oil Infrastructure	1,620
Other Targets	8,233
TOTAL	**26,374**

forces." A general should have said, right there, against all doctrine, "we don't do it." They're doing it anyway.

They are using rebel forces on the ground, indigenous forces, they call them—sounds scientific. It has nothing to do with jointness: There is no common military culture, there is no common language, there are no common procedures, there is no force coherence. It's just two different things happening. The Kurds and all the good guys are on the ground trying to do something, and the air war is taking place on top of them. Not very

professional.

Waging war by air power alone—and in the last 25 years America and NATO have done it in several countries—is useless. It's just useless. [**Slide 6**]

Air War's Death Sentences

And now, the knockout argument: Ethics. Rebels and insurgents will always avoid big military engagements. They will mingle with the population. They do this deliberately. If you, with all your precision, and all your thorough targeting, try to hit terrorists in Aleppo, or in Ar-Raqqah, you will hit civilians. Now, I ask you, how many children are we willing to kill, for one terrorist? I say: None. [**Slide 7**] [applause]

In the air headquarters in Qatar, in the planning process, there is a legal adviser. NATO has one, the French have one, the Germans have one, a legal adviser, a lawyer who will tell the planner how many civilians a certain target is "worth." He writes death sentences: He will say, 20? No. 10? OK. This happens every day, and we just don't care. I think that's a scandal. [**Slide 8**] [applause]

How Do We Get to a New Paradigm?

Now, to my last point: How can we get rid of the old paradigm of making war? How can we get to a new one? I think it's a cultural change, and cultural changes do not work from above. That's dictatorship; we have tried this before. To make a cultural change

from below is the guillotine; we have seen that before. It can only work when people learn. And learning can only happen when you try to incite discourses, inform people, encourage them to say "no." Ask the politicians, ask the generals these three questions about aims, ethics, and of course, military ways of doing things.

So, my plea is for getting away from a paradigm of waging war for political reasons; we should wage war *only* for humanitarian reasons.

MARCO ZANNI

The Collapse of the European Financial System

Marco Zanni, MEP for the Italian Five Star Movement (M5S), is the head of the M5S delegation in the Economic and Monetary Affairs Committee of the European Parliament. He has introduced several Glass-Steagall resolutions in the European Parliament and has visited U.S. Congressmen to push for action on Glass-Steagall legislation. He titled his June 25 address, "The Collapse of the European Financial System and the Failure of the Banking Union."

Good afternoon everyone, and many thanks to the Schiller Institute for the opportunity to speak on the situation of the European Union and of the European financial system.

Briefly, before assessing the status of the European economy and financial system, let me say a couple of words about what happened on Friday, the surprising result of the UK referendum on its membership in the European Union. As I say, the result was "surprising" and a very strong message of democracy to the European Union and to the European institutions. The European Union ignored the will of peoples and citizens, in forcing a political integration that is not the right way for Europe to cooperate. I remember referenda in 2005 that rejected the European Constitution, in France and the Netherlands, and I remember in 2008, the referendum in Ireland on the Lisbon Treaty. The European institutions decided to ignore the voice of the citizens and Brexit is the result of this lack of a political view for a united Europe with cooperation among European countries.

I think that this is a huge opportunity for European countries to sit together around the table, to assess and declare the failure of this project of the European Union, and try to set up together a new project, an alternative project for Europe; because Europe is different from the European Union, and I am a strong supporter of Europe

and of European citizens. [applause] And as I was saying, to try to create an alternative project for Europe that will restore economic growth in Europe, that will respect the differences that European countries have, and in a framework of real cooperation. So, a Europe focussed on the real needs of the real economy, of small and medium enterprises, and not a Europe based on the needs of speculation, of finance and of big banks, as this European Union is doing.

I received very good news just an hour ago: The European Commissioner responsible for financial regulation, former lobbyist in Brussels for the financial system, Mr. Jonathan Hill [Commissioner for Financial Stability, Financial Services, and Capital Markets Union] has resigned as a result of the Brexit. So this is good news; let's resolve that we can all work better on economic and monetary affairs inside the European Parliament.

Upside-Down World of the ECB

I will try to assess and present the status of the European financial system. As the title of this panel points out very well: "The European financial system is collapsing." It is collapsing because of wrong policies brought about by European governments and by the European Union. After the financial crisis in 2008, the European Union decided to focus on the wrong problems. So they tried to set up financial regulations focussed on trying to overcome the *consequences* of a crisis.

In my view, this is not the right way to restore, and to guarantee the stability of the financial system. If we want a banking system, a financial system that is safe, if we want financial stability, we should focus regulations on *preventing* financial crises. Working and regulating the liability and equity side of banks is not the right way; we have to focus on the asset side, on the exposure of the financial system to certain types of financial assets. In this way and in this task the European Union failed, and the project of the banking union failed.

Let me talk about the first pillar of the banking union, that is, the single supervisory mechanism for all of the participating member states of the banking union, for the banking systems of the member states. The approach to single supervision delivered by the European Central Bank (ECB), or by a branch of the ECB, is completely wrong, and the evidence of this is in the stress tests presented by the ECB after November 2014.

The mistake in the analysis and approach of the ECB is that it assesses only major risks contained in the balance sheets of the European banking system. It completely failed in assessing the exposure to problematic, speculative financial assets that are contained in the balance sheets of the system. I am talking about what the regulation calls "Level 3 assets." Level 3 assets are financial assets that are illiquid, so that the price and the figure that is posted on the balance sheet on the assets side of a bank is decided by an internal model prepared by the same banks, whose interest is to set a certain figure for the value of these assets. The single supervisory mechanism decided not to assess and not to consider the risk related to Level 3 derivatives exposure of the European banking system, and this is a *huge* mistake that is threatening the stability of the system.

According to the stress tests and analysis of the ECB, a bank like Intesa San Paolo, one of the most important Italian banks, has problems. I know that Intesa San Paolo has problems on the nonperforming loans (NPL) side, on the credit risk side. But 80% of Intesa San Paolo's assets related to credit, are related to the real economy, and just 20% of its exposure is related to speculative financial instruments, to trading and so on. According to the ECB, this bank is riskier than Deutsche Bank or the BNP Paribas bank, for example. But looking at the balance sheets of Deutsche Bank and BNP Paribas, the proportion on the asset side is completely the opposite: They have exposure of 80% of their assets to Level 3 assets, to derivatives, to speculative instruments, to trading assets, and just 20% of the assets are dedicated to the real economy.

I think a system that considers Intesa San Paolo riskier than Deutsche Bank or BNP Paribas is completely wrong and is threatening the stability of the European Union, of European countries, and of the European financial system. The single supervisory mechanism is unfair, because it fails to assess the market risk, and also the level risk on the balance sheets

of banks. All of those too-big-to-fail banks, all those speculative banks, are facing billionaire legal actions due to their behavior in the financial markets: They manipulated the exchange rate markets, they manipulated the interest rate markets, and they are facing billions in fines that could threaten the stability of bank balance sheets. And the ECB is not assessing this risk, deliberately. This is a political decision.

Further Financialization Is No Answer

By looking at what is happening in the Italian banking system, we see the evidence of the inequity of this approach. Italian banks have problems related to the exposure to NPLs, but it is, I say usually, an "error-induced crisis," because if your economy shrinks, if your small and medium-sized enterprises go into bankruptcy, if your homeowners cannot pay their mortgages, borrowers cannot pay mortgages, clearly the banking system will suffer a huge exposure to NPLs. If your economy is not performing well, you will experience problems in the credit market and problems related to the NPLs.

Now, as I say, this crisis, these problems, are related to the euro in my view, because the single currency is creating huge macroeconomic imbalances between European countries. The Eurozone is an optimized currency area, and I think that due to political constraints and due to huge differences between eurozone countries, we cannot fix this currency union. So this is the problem related to the euro.

What about the policies that the European Union is trying to set up to make the financial system safer, more stable? It's all related to more financialization of the system. Just one example: On a policy proposed by the former commissioner for financial regulation, they think that if we need to restore growth in the European Union, we have to revive securitization. So the proposal that now is on the table in the European Union, in the European Parliament, is a framework for a simple, transparent, and standardized securitization. That is meaningless. Because, looking at the proposal, there is nothing simple, nothing transparent, and nothing standardized about securitization. If you use synthetic securitization, if you use derivatives, collateralized debt obligations (CDOs), there is no simple securitization. And securitization is not the means to restore funding for the real economy.

Europe's Role in the New World Economy

We have proposals in the European Parliament to restore growth and the stability of the financial system— clearly a first step. We have proposed one bill in the Italian Parliament and one in the European Parliament, in the framework of the banking structural reform, for restoring banking separation. We think that we have to set up a sort of modern, European Glass-Steagall that will simplify the regulation of the banking system, and will make separation between the core part of a bank and a speculative bank, in order to create a banking system that is no more focussed on speculation in the financial system, but on the needs of the real economy, on the needs of people. And this is the first step. [applause]

The second step is a proposal related to one of the most troubled banks in the European Union, that is, Monte dei Paschi di Siena. I think you all know the situation of the third Italian bank, the oldest bank in Europe. Monte dei Paschi di Siena was founded in the 15th century and operated throughout the centuries to support the real economy.

Now we have the opportunity—the Italian government has the opportunity—to take over this bank that is really in trouble, and make it an example of what could be a banking system focussed on the real economy. So we are proposing to nationalize Monte dei Paschi di Siena. The Italian Treasury is already the main shareholder, with a 4% stake. We are proposing to set up a clear mission for Monte dei Paschi di Siena, in order to have the bank focus clearly on the needs of the real economy. We will not allow it to operate in trading business, to operate in the derivatives business. Its mission will be just to operate as a public service for credit, in order to support the real economy.

I think that this proposal could be a benchmark for Europe, for the European banking system. We have to do more in the European Parliament, and I hope that after Mr. Hill, we will be able to talk again about the banking structural reform and the European Glass-Steagall that this lobbyist blocked, after being elected commissioner, and then go on with a project for Europe, a project that will overcome this failure of the European Union and will bring Europe again to the center of the global scenario as a connection between the United States and Asia. I think that this is a good way for Europe to restore growth, to restore democracy, and to take the role that European citizens and European people should have in the global scenario.

DAISUKE KOTEGAWA

Japan's Outlook Concerning Eurasian Cooperation

Daisuke Kotegawa is the research director of the Canon Institute for Global Studies, Japan. At the IMF, he was the Executive Director for Japan. For 35 years, he worked in the Ministry of Finance. He addressed the Schiller Institute conference in Berlin on June 25.

I'd like to divide my presentation into four parts. The first one is very short, about myself, why I'm here. The second part is about the Japanese economy, with specific focus upon three points which were actually asked by Helga. And the third part is my observa-

tion about the world economy, from my own personal perspective. In the fourth part—just inspired by Mr. LaRouche's point—I would like to explain a very, very important new invention which my company created very recently which would completely change this world.

First, about myself. I worked in the Ministry of Finance of Japan for 35 years, and fortunately, or unfortunately, I was in charge of the settlement of the financial crisis in the late 1990s in Japan. I lost some friends of mine and my staff, as well as my friends, Japanese bankers who were arrested and put in jail or committed suicide. But I survived.

At that time I had to liquidate major Japanese investment banks, two companies—Yamaichi Securities and another—and also I had to partially nationalize two major banks in Japan. In 2007 I went to the IMF, and I was involved in the liquidation of Lehman Brothers in 2008. Just last week, I had a chance to meet my former colleague, Mr. Dominique Strauss-Kahn, in St. Petersburg at the Economic Forum. That's my background.

Prospects for Russo-Japanese Rapprochement

My second part is about the Japanese economy, and my first focus is upon the relationship between Japan and Russia. Last month on May 2, I celebrated my birthday; it was a joint birthday party with my friend who is a very famous Russian conductor, Valery Gergiev, because his birthday is May 2nd, and mine is May 3rd. So for the last seven years, we have celebrated our birthdays together somewhere in the world. [applause] And he told me that he would perform on the next day in Kazan, and in Yekaterinburg on May 4th. But he didn't say anything further. On May 5th, I was sitting in a lounge in the Moscow Airport and suddenly I saw his face, performing in Syria at Aleppo! That was a big surprise, but that was a fantastic performance.

Also at that birthday party of about 40 people, I had my friend, my very good friend who is the best speaker of the Russian language—he is our ambassador in Moscow. Early in the morning of the next day, he flew to Sochi to support our Prime Minister Mr. Abe in his meeting with Mr. Putin. That meeting took place on May 6th. On May 7th I received an email from my friend. He said three things: Oh, I cannot tell you anything specific. Number 2, Meeting went very well. Number 3, Prime Minister went back to Japan with full satisfaction. [laughter] So, that was a very simple message.

But thanks to that message,—As you know, in 2018 in Russia, they have their Presidential election, and also in China they have this kind of election next year; usually one year before that kind of election, nothing moves because people are more concerned about where they're going to work on something.

So we had thought it was not likely that we would have a final agreement with Russia next year. But this meeting on May 6 changed everything. Now, we expect that our Prime Minister, Mr. Abe, is likely to accept the invitation of Mr. Putin, and will attend the economic forum in Vladivostok on Sept. 2-3, and I am quite hopeful that within this year, Mr. Putin will come to Japan. [applause] And if that will happen, it is highly likely that we would come to the final agreement with Russia sometime next year. Now, I think I'm very optimistic about it. So that part is now going very well.

More Nuclear Power for Japan

Japan's plans for nuclear power are an important point. As you know, we shut down all nuclear power plants after the incident at Fukushima in 2011. Last year, finally, we reactivated two of them. And then followed by one. But two weeks ago, our Ministry of Economy made public the report which provides the prospect for the future energy combination in Japan; the target year is 2030, and in that report, we expect that we will build 24 new nuclear power plants in Japan. [applause]

Japan's Tsunami of Chinese Tourists

My third point is that the Japanese economy is actually now in a kind of bubble that is not shown in figures. Instead, I'd like to just tell you about the incredible incidents now in Tokyo. We relaxed some visa requirements for people from Southeast Asia. Of course, we didn't relax visa requirements for the Chinese, because we are afraid that if we did that, several hundred million Chinese might come to Tokyo.

But last year, we received 5 million Chinese tourists. That was a 100% increase over two years ago. And the average purchase volume of each Chinese tourist is now something about $3,000. So now we have a shortfall of hotels. After the big earthquake and tsunami in 2011, hotels in Tokyo had vacancy rates of about 90%—miserable. But these days everything is full. Especially starting last year, Chinese people started to come to Japan—at the end of March and early April—just to enjoy the cherry blossoms in Tokyo! So now, all those parks that are very famous for their cherry blossoms in Tokyo, are completely occupied by Chinese tourists.

Because of the shortfall in hotels, starting last year—also in local cities, where the size of the population is something like Frankfurt am Main, and another something like Wiesbaden—they started to receive huge numbers of Chinese tourists. So they set up a fleet from Shanghai to those cities; last year a ship with 2,000 Chinese tourists came in, followed by another ship with 3,000. And this year, in a very small city, something like Wiesbaden, they received a *very* big ship with a capacity of 8,000 tourists!

As you can imagine, you need to have at least one bus for 100 tourists. In the first case, we had 20 buses and 30 buses; this year they had to arrange for 80 buses for those people. And they stayed on the ship! So thanks to those foreign tourists, our economy is now very good. [laughter]

Infrastructure, not Investment Bankers, OK?

Mr. LaRouche talked about infrastructure, and I am very thankful for his comment, because as Deputy Budget Examiner in the Ministry of Finance, I was in charge of the budget of Japanese economic assistance to China. In 1989, we agreed upon economic assistance to China of more than $10 billion each year for six years. So those loans were made to build, for example, an airport in Beijing, an airport in Shanghai, an airport in Guangzhou, and seven ports and seven railroads, and seven fertilizer factories, seven dams, and seven power plants. And also the phone network in Shanghai, as well as the phone network in Beijing, and the subway system in Beijing, were built with these loans, which were carried on 0.5% interest.

Thanks to that infrastructure, Japanese companies started to make investments in China, and now we are actually getting the fruits in the form of huge numbers of Chinese tourists.

So I'm very sure that if we just make investments in the right way, we can actually redouble the volume of demand which is completely missing in this world. And I completely agree with Mr. Zanni's opinion, because we don't care about investment bankers. They do care only about rich people, OK? And they are interested in only gambling, and we don't need them. But we *do* need commercial banks, because they are the settlement bankers and they take care of deposits. [applause] To stop investment bankers gambling, as he said, it is very important to look at the asset side. Even if we would allow bankers to keep a huge amount of money under the name of equity, it does not stop gamblers from gambling.

So we have to separate these two, and we have to take all banks back to our own life. And he just men-

tioned—of course, this a little bit difficult to understand—but there is a concept of "notional amount" for derivatives. When they gamble, they need some kind of base figure, which is not real. But it is said that the notional amount of derivatives held by Deutsche Bank is €300 *trillion*! That is five times larger than the GNP of Germany! So you'll be really frightened. But don't worry: There's a way to settle it. Those investment bankers, they just gamble against each other; maybe the counterpart might be Goldman Sachs or Morgan Stanley. So, they should just net out everything. Then suddenly, the amount would become almost zero; so here again, we don't have to worry about it. And we should focus more upon manufacturing.

And so now's the time to disclose our invention: It is a small cooking machine the size of an electric range. [Kotegawa explains in detail that the machine cooks without allowing the food any access to oxygen. The food is therefore not oxidized, which is very good for health, and keeps the food very tasty.]

Every Day Counts In Today's Showdown To Save Civilization

That's why you need EIR's **Daily Alert Service**, a strategic overview compiled with the input of Lyndon LaRouche, and delivered to your email 5 days a week.

For example: On Jan. 7, EIR's Daily Alert featured the British hand behind the pattern of global provocations toward war. Of special note is British Intelligence's role in instigating the Saudi Kingdom's attempt to set off a Sunni-Shia war. This religious war has been the intent of British strategy since the Blair-Bush attack on Iraq in 2003.

We also uniquely update you regularly on the progress toward the release of the suppressed 28 pages of the Congressional Inquiry on 9/11, which would expose the Saudi role.

Every edition highlights the reality of the impending financial crash/bail-in policies that would realize the British goal of mass depopulation.

This is intelligence you need to act on, if we are going to survive as a nation and a species. Can you really afford to be without it?

THURSDAY, JANUARY 7, 2016

Volume 2, Number 97

EIR Daily Alert Service

P.O. Box 17390, Washington, DC 20041-0390

- British Crown Pushing War and Genocide in 2016
- Financial Mudslide Goes On; Monetarist Tyranny Gloats over Bail-Ins
- Moody's Downgrades Portugal's Novo Banco
- Puerto Rico's Default: It's Every Vulture for Himself
- Wide Glass-Steagall Debate Set Off Again by Sanders Speech
- MI6 Mouthpiece Evans-Pritchard Touts Persian Gulf Chaos
- North Korea Tests a Miniaturized Hydrogen Bomb
- Uighur Terrorists Found in Indonesia
- Foreign Investors Are Flocking In to China

EDITORIAL

British Crown Pushing War and Genocide in 2016

✂

Who Is Sylvia?

by Dennis Speed

July 5—Lyndon LaRouche's "Manhattan Project" to restore Hamilton's Presidency to the United States by removing the "presidential pretense" that is the Obama Administration from power, is on a daily basis actively deliberating upon the following problem with thousands of people in the metropolitan area: "Is it possible, in a time of crisis such as this one, to avoid our impending national suicide?" The capacity of nations and empires for indifferent, sometimes sudden, and even festive self-destruction seems boundless, as it does in the trans-Atlantic sector today, an apparently uncontrollable societal compulsion.

Far more civilizations have failed than have succeeded in human history. Is that about to become our fate as well? Does the principle of self-government through human creativity, the shadow of which is cast in the Preamble of the United States Constitution and the first sections of the Declaration of Independence, provide a sufficient basis for some set of Americans, who are simultaneously United States patriots as well as world-citizens, to change the fate about to be thrust upon us by the scythe of history? Could that fate not be avoided by America in the same way that Edgar Poe's protagonist avoided his, in Poe's famous story, "The Pit and the Pendulum"—by thinking creatively?

How might we out-think our assumptions, our "virtual reality" axioms, and survive by rejecting the sad inevitability of our present Obama-delivered course to thermonuclear extinction? Götterdämmerung —"the twilight of the gods"—is not "ordained" or "predestined" to occur. That is an anti-human notion: only Wagnerians need be condemned to that fate. Cultural

EIRNS/Robert Baker

The Schiller Institute Chorus conducted by Diane Sare, with tenor soloist Everett Suttle singing the spiritual "Great Day."

EIRNS/Stuart Lewis

William Warfield, Sylvia Olden Lee, and George Shirley (left to right), at the May 28, 1999 National Music Conference "For a Marian Anderson National Conservatory of Music Movement" at Rankin Chapel, Howard University.

suicide has, throughout most history, merely been "ordained" by cultures that have, often decades before, and often willfully so, lost their moral fitness to survive.

Especially viewing, at this stage, the prospects that presently surround the U. S. Trump/Clinton-dominated Presidential electoral process, the only recourse available now is, as one New York City radio preacher's punch-line puts it: "It's time to pray." There is a caveat. In the words of the Psalmist of the Old Testament: "How can we sing the Lord's song in a foreign land?" Axioms must fall for a truly human solution to arise in the mind. "Obama cannot be immediately and lawfully removed from control of the Presidency" is such an axiom.

On Sunday June 26, the New York Schiller Institute Community Chorus participated in a memorial tribute to the extraordinary vocal coach, pianist, and pedagogue, Sylvia Olden Lee, the first African-American contracted at the Metropolitan Opera of New York (1954), and a former member of the Schiller Institute Advisory Board. Lee, who died in 2004, worked with the Schiller Institute from 1993 until her death. She would have been 99 years old this June 29. (The Foundation for the Revival of Classical Culture, which has in the past three years championed the principle of restoring "proper tuning"— not higher or lower, but scientific tuning which preserves and strengthens human vocal production though Italian bel canto training and performance—co-sponsored the event. Foundation board member and conduc-

tor Tony Morss also gave a presentation there.) The combination symposium and musical program, particularly its concluding half, was a successful attempt to pose a resolution to the dilemma posed in Psalm 137:4. The "strange land" of arbitrary and irrational demands placed on singers by artificially high tunings has been an area of interest and combat for three decades now, and is central to every other problem of education of our time.

Drama as Music

The audience was placed in a dramatic setting that began with Sylvia addressing it directly— through a videotaped extemporaneous presentation she had given in February of 1994 to a conference of the Schiller Institute, at the time that Lyndon LaRouche had just days earlier been released from prison. (LaRouche had been unjustly incarcerated for five years, from January 1989 until January 1994.)

Following the video, Elvira Green, recently retired artist-in-residence at North Carolina Central College, and Diane Sare, founder and director of the New York Schiller Institute Community chorus, evoked the spirit and person of Sylvia Lee in short reminiscences about her character and her work.

Sylvia often said that the initials of her name, the same as that of her mother, stood for "Save Young Lyric Voices In Advance." Her "Project SYLVIA" converged on work that the Schiller Institute had pioneered in the mid-1980s, at the instigation of Lyndon LaRouche, on returning the Classical music world to the proper tuning at C=256 cycles per second. This was the "human tuning" used by Bach, Mozart, Haydn, Beethoven, Schubert, Brahms, Verdi, Dvorak, et al., as opposed to the raising of the pitch by the likes of Nazi propaganda minister Joseph Goebbels during the late 1930s.

The crime committed against musicians, particularly vocalists, of arbitrary tuning "for artistic brilliance" goes largely unreported, and even largely unnoticed; that is exactly how, and why, "young lyric voices" find themselves battered, destroyed, and discarded. Maestro Anthony Morss, recently retired from a career of orchestral conducting since 1959, provided

Some of the participants in the musical portion of the program (right to left): Elvira Green, Everett Suttle, Frank Mathis, and accompanist Robert Wilson.

a most in-depth, needed "backgrounder" to the concert audience on the battle to restore principle to Classical music. In fact, it is exactly the inability to stand up for principle in this matter, as the Schiller Institute did in 1988 with the release of its *Manual on Tuning and Registration*, that accounts for the horrendous decline in familiarity with Classical music among youth today in the United States and Europe.

The "musical" portion of the program then commenced. Without the "pre-musical" sections, however, the intent of the whole tribute to Sylvia would have been inaccessible to the audience. The use of a choral, multi-voiced prologue, including Sylvia's own voice, conveyed the intent, and appeared to have accomplished the effect desired.

Elvira Green provided the "invocation," performing the Spiritual "City Called Heaven" unaccompanied. Three Spirituals, "Go Down, Moses" (arranged by Sylvia Lee), "Come Out De Wilderness" (traditional), and "My Lord, What A Morning" (arranged by Harry T. Burleigh) were then performed by the Schiller Institute New York Community Chorus, conducted by Diane Sare.

Several individual musical selections, all of which Lee had coached singers in through the decades, were performed: "Ev'ry Valley Shall Be Exhalted" (tenor John Sigerson), "Ritorna vincitor" (soprano Indira Mahajan), "Mon coeur s'ouvre a ta voix" and "O Rest in the Lord" (mezzo-soprano Mary Phillips), "Lensky's Aria" (tenor Everett Suttle), "The Lark" (baritone Frank Mathis), "Dio, che nell'alma infondere" (Suttle/Mathis), "Du bist die Ruh'" (soprano Michelle Fuchs), "Adelaide" (Sigerson), "Plegaria (Los tres amores)," (Suttle), "Que te importa que no venga" and "Anch'io dischiuso un giorno" (soprano Rosa D'Imperio). The chorus and soloists then sang Verdi's "Va, pensiero" from the opera *Nabucco* to conclude.

Tragedy and Discovery

Now the audience was prepared to listen to the "discovery" they were about to be caused to make: *The Life of Christ*, a song cycle composed, with narration, by Roland Hayes, one of the greatest artists ever produced by the United States. A twenty-minute intermission gave the audience time to prepare themselves, and also allowed those not prepared to "journey to the upper room" to leave. *The Life of Christ* consists of ten songs, with Roland Hayes-authored narration preceding each selection. The singer—or in this case, singers—have the option to add other pieces, as Hayes himself did, where appropriate. In this case, two were added by Everett Suttle and Frank Mathis, who generally alternated. Hayes' narrative continuity was performed by Elvira Green. Green had personally worked with Roland Hayes on several of these very Spirituals, as had Sylvia Lee. Since Hayes had himself learned how these Spirituals were to be performed from his mother, who had grown up as a slave on a Georgia plantation (which plantation Hayes, once he had made a career, later purchased as a home for his mother), the tradition of Spirituals singing that was being presented to that audience was directly taken from their original mode of performance.

Selections seven, eight and nine—"The Last Supper," "They Led My Lord Away," and "He Never Said a Mumberlin' Word," were the turning point, not only in the song cycle, but in the entire day's performance. Performers, narrator, and even audience became one, directly hearing, in the unaccompanied "He Never Said," the scene of Christ's crucifixion transposed onto the stage of their imagination. This is a moment rarely achieved in musical performance, and is the inner force of what usually goes by the name "prayer" for lack of a better term. Hayes prefaced this piece: "In respect both to its music and to its marvelous words, this song is a master work among all Aframerican religious folk songs. It definitely was the creation of an African who came to these shores already an accomplished bard. This particular version is a song sermon, emphatically a solo. He whom this poet-musician so poignantly reveres in this song *is the only being he would call master*."

It was reaching this point, this discovery, simultaneously shared by one hundred other minds, of a previously unknown "continent of the spirit," Percy Shelley's "everlasting universe of things" that "flows through the mind," the most profound type of human experience— "the land that speaks my language"—for the which all the other effort of the day had been made. The audience "instinctively" recognized that it had been brought to a new level, to higher ground, which was displayed in the sudden and deep silence of mental absorption that enveloped the performance. That had been achieved by using what *appeared* to be the most simple tool of the Classical musical repertoire—the unaccompanied, trained single human voice. All the greatest composers of history, known and unknown, Western and non-Western would, however, have known otherwise.

The artists used the conclusion of *The Life of Christ* to reinforce this moment of discovery, with an unaccompanied performance of the Spiritual, "Were You There When They Crucified My Lord?" This was performed by Elvira Green, who interpolated a change in the text, unplanned by her: she changed the refrain "Were you there" in her last verse to "You *are* there"!

Asked about this the next day, she reported that as she sang, she discussed with Hayes and Sylvia whether this would be right to do, "and I got Roland's permission." So the idea "you are there," at that moment, in that setting, was, as in all great uses of metaphor, a si-multaneous reference to the text, to Hayes, to the audience, to Christ, and to Sylvia Lee. Green ended the program as she had begun it, simultaneously inside and outside of the concert program itself, acting as chorus for the event as a whole.

The "chorus proper," the Schiller Institute Chorus, with Everett Suttle as the tenor soloist, then sang the Spiritual, "Great Day." The exiting audience appeared to agree with the Spiritual's outlook.

'What's This Got to Do with Reality?'

Americans claim to be powerless to use the Constitutional power of impeachment, yet still pretend to be free, even though the murderers that carried out the 9/11 attack, specifically their Saudi and British components, still operate with impunity. Is our population so terrorized by the "drone presidency" of Barack Obama, that it would rather escape *from* freedom rather than fight *for* it? It is only by developing the ability to experience true freedom through art, and the ability to convey that sense of true freedom through artistic performance—the task of the Schiller Institute as a chorus, and as an organization—that we are likely to provide the nation with the "ganas"—the desire—to win against tyranny.

In his essay, "On the Use of the Chorus in Tragedy," poet and historian Friedrich Schiller states: "True art… does not aim for a mere temporary play: it seriously intends not to transpose a person into a merely momentary dream of freedom, but to make him really and in fact free, and to accomplish this by awakening in him a force, exercising it and developing it, to thrust the sensuous world, which otherwise only presses upon us as crude material, bearing down upon us as a blind power, into an objective distance, to transpose it into a free work of our mind, and to achieve mastery over the material with ideas."

The Schiller Institute is experimenting with this same principle of the employment of the chorus on our present national tragedy, in today's Manhattan. Succeeding, as Aeschylus did through Greek drama and music, in teaching our present-day Athenians that "there are no gods living on Mount Olympus" is the first step in preparing Americans to defeat the British "empire of the mind" that holds them hostage, placing the shackles on themselves at night. Alexander Hamilton opposed slavery, used his mind, and built a national republic, with Manhattan as its capital. Can we demand anything less of ourselves, if we would keep it?

Sylvia Olden Lee Speaks

by Dennis Speed

July 4—Sylvia Lee's family background, and her own work, including original research on the history of African-American music that spanned 375 years, is a focal point of the American national experience, at its best and worst. In February of 1994, she spoke extemporaneously to a Schiller Institute conference about "Who is Sylvia?" To fill out that picture, we have added more of her own words, taken from the book, *The Memoirs of Sylvia Olden Lee.*

You lovely, beleaguered people!... I was applauded so much for what I did yesterday, and I want you to just really think about it. I would be no good were it not for the fact that I am accompanying soloists who, whether their *accompaniment* was good or not, you're not paying attention to it. You are listening to the message that does come from the singers. We had Bob McFerrin—he's incomparable. And also, he's a Fisk-ite [alumnus of Fisk University].

Mr. Roland Hayes... I got to know almost from birth. [I] had a meeting with him five or six months before his death [in 1977]. [I] did some work with him—he told me exactly how to do Angel Mo's songs [Hayes' mother, a former slave in Georgia]. And he and daddy stood as tenors elbow to elbow for five long years at Fisk University as half of the Fisk quartet. And Hayes' daughter is here, and I

EIRNS/Stuart Lewis

Sylvia Olden Lee addressing the Feb. 18-21, 1994 Schiller Institute conference music panel, in Washington, D.C.

guess you've learned that already. Afrika is here....

The father is just indescribable... He was the soul of dignity, and ethics, and truth and reality—no nonsense—and was a dignified prince all the time. He, who reached the heights 'way back in the 20s and 30s, of the Carnegie Hall and higher level, and went abroad and was decorated by so many of the crowned heads. He sang with a dedication and a special message from several languages, at least five: and you never got the idea that "well, he has nice pronunciation." No! He had a message with everything he sang. So he did Bach, and Schütz, and Debussy, and the French, Italian, and German for which he deserved every bit of the credit that he got. Then, most of the time, I don't know about all of the time, but he certainly did include *his* songs, and did *them* with dignity. There was nothing patronizing about it— "And I have now risen higher and it's so nice to remember my people's songs"—none of that. This was another message. And he said for all of us to recognize, along with the Classics, to never forget that the songs of people were real and to do them, no matter whether dialect—and you *know* that all Negro Spirituals are not in dialect. There are some that are very, very straightforward—to sing them with dignity, and without making a travesty of them: to think deeply, and to do the very best you could.

Now, I am speaking from a Fisk family to which I never belonged, because I am the granddaughter of a slave....

Sylvia's Background

Sylvia discussed this aspect of her background in great detail in her *Memoirs*, which we interpolate here:

Grandpa was born in 1845 and belonged to the Oldham plantation near Louisville. He was fifteen or sixteen years old when the war broke out, and he ran away from the plantation through the woods to the border of Kentucky and Ohio. You couldn't travel in the day, so he just hiked it by cover of darkness to the Ohio River, and swam over at the point where it's only a creek. Since he was too young and scrawny to fight as a soldier with the Union Army, they made him a water boy. But eventually things got really bad, and they gave him a gun. Then Mr. Lincoln came forth, and freed everybody in 1863. After the War, Grandpa went off back home. He needed a name and thought: "Oldham was a pretty decent master, so I'll take his name. But I'm not going to spell it that darn way. I'll be George *Olden*."...

My paternal great-grandfather, Nelson G. Merry, was also born a slave. When they said to his Cherokee mother: "You've got to get out of here and make your way to Oklahoma," she gathered her eleven or twelve kids together and was forced to march on that Trail of Tears in the winter of 1838-1839, from South Carolina westwards to the reservations. (I didn't know until recently that Indians were slaves. If you were a whole Indian, or half-Indian, or married to one, you could be enslaved.)

When great-great-grandmother got to Nashville, she declared: "I'm not going any farther, and they can't make me." She just squatted there, and the kids were sold to different people.

My great-grandfather, who was born in 1824, was bought by a kindly old couple who liked him from the beginning. When he was sixteen, his widowed mistress, Betsy Merry, died and willed him to the First Baptist Church, where he

served as sexton. The pastor went against the law, and taught him how to read and write. In 1845, he was freed, and eight years later, became Nashville's first ordained Negro Baptist Minister. Great-grandfather became official pastor of the First Colored Baptist Church, which eventually numbered over two thousand members... and was the leader of the civil rights movement....

My daughter, Eve, got her doctorate in German from Vanderbilt, and before she returned her robe to the renters, I said, "You're going to go by our great great grandpa's church here, honey, and have your picture taken smiling up at him. If he'd shown up at Vanderbilt in those days, he would've had to have a mop and broom."

Sylvia's Schiller conference speech continued:

My grandfather lived long enough for me to get to know him, so you know that makes me absolutely Jurassic! But I got to know my grandfather... He came up to Fisk and met my grandmother, who was fortunate, because her father was the founder of the Baptist Church still standing, 1853. She was the daughter of the minister, and a [Fisk] Jubilee singer, one of the first. She did not go abroad and get her portrait painted by Victoria's portraitist, because her father drew the line: "No daughter of mine is going traipsing all over foreign countries." So she couldn't go. She married George Olden, and then they had my father, who was a theologian—he was studying for the ministry. But he belonged to this quartet, the Fisk Quartet people. Roland Hayes was the only one [of them] that was a music major. The rest of them—Dr. Wesley, the later president of Wilberforce [College], was a Classics major, and Lem Foster was a sociologist... Even though they had their pursuits, if you were a Fisk Quartet person, you couldn't just get up and throw a few Spirituals around—because it was quite easy for them to sing [them]. They're close to the atmosphere all around. Fisk is built on the spirit of the Spiritual. They had jobs every other Saturday to get up early and go [by] horse and buggy into the wilds—that's true—of Tennessee, bring-

Sylvia Olden Lee, working with student vocalists at an April 2002 master class in Kulas Recital Hall at Oberlin University.

ing back new Spirituals. But every one of the members of that quartet also had to study lieder, chansons, canzoni. They had to study voice technique, they had to know piano, and they had to know how to read. So they had to add to what they had as a curriculum, and get up and perform Classical pieces.

First Accompanying

My father and Dr. Wesley, at many an NAACP meeting, in the teens and 20s, sang. [If] They needed a musical interlude, Daddy and Charlie got up and did the duet from *La Forza del destino*.... So my first accompaniment: I started very early, and by the time I was eight Daddy was doing a little of his leftover Classics. I remember my first accompanying was to accompany him in "Du bist die Ruh'" of Schubert. And then, when I got ambitious, he said, "Do 'Hark! Hark! The Lark'"! So I worked very hard at that. I was eight years old, and it was in the key of C, so all I had to do was put some time to it. I remember it very well. Later, in all these long years, we journeyed, my family, my husband and two children, we went to München—Munich—for only one year. But it ended up, it was seven.... Bonn had asked our consulate if

we knew of anybody who could do a whole program of Spirituals.

And I asked every Negro/Colored/African-American who was there if he would consent to do it, they had a tour ready. And nobody wanted to do this. So I thought of going to the head of USIA and saying, "You know you folks"—he was white—"you think that anything that isn't Spirituals is jazz, or something, but we have a full ledger of offerings creatively for vocal singing. Why don't you let me get an anthology [program] starting with the African chant, unaccompanied, and coming with the earliest Spirituals—1619-1630—and bring it on around to the work songs, play songs, the street cries, which you know are so wonderful, to creole songs, and then to our art songs. It has been found, lately, there are more than one thousand composers, Black composers of serious music... So as soon as we would get this program together and go, they would always ask us, or quite frequently, "Could you possibly come back next week, because we've turned away a whole auditorium?" There were also published over a dozen editions of Negro Spirituals in Germany, with the German translation. And they would have us come and sing the original, and then teach them how to do the Spiritual in their language. And after we had gotten through with "There is a balm in Gilead," one of the folks walked up and said, "Your know, this has no African sound to me. It seems quite like Schubert." And I said, Well, that would naturally happen, if the masters loved music and had to have it—they had live music only—and they would find the most talented of the slaves and train them as well as they could, and have them to entertain, so that they would have them go around and hear other music, and hear the Classics... Many a Spiritual has an Eighteenth-Nineteenth Century patina that goes through it. There are some of them that are still tribal, and I have a list of about 300, and they are different kinds. Some of them are quite martial, and you can hear the tom-toms in them, and others are very tuneful and sound about like "Danny Boy." And it only shows that we are closer and closer, if we all will work very, very diligently.

I know from the fact that you are here—your

presence attests to the fact that you believe in justice and one world. I hope you keep persevering and going into the far corners of this globe selling it to people, because we *are one family*. We belong to one God, no matter what you call Him. And as such, we should keep in touch with each other through Classical and folk music.

GREGORY HOPKINS

Reminiscence on Sylvia Olden Lee

The following is a statement from tenor, conductor, and keyboardist Gregory Hopkins, a longtime professional associate of Sylvia Olden Lee, on the occasion of the June 26 "birthday" musical tribute celebrated in her honor in New York. Mr. Hopkins currently serves as the Artistic Director for the Harlem Opera Theater.

I met Mrs. Lee when I was eighteen years old. I was a freshman at Temple University and singing in the put-together chorus of priests for Opera Ebony's debut production of *Aida* in Philadelphia. Once we came together with the conductor, Everett Lee, who was her husband, she became the rehearsal pianist and coach. She heard my voice in the chorus, where I was marking the lead tenor in the rehearsals, and said: "There's the voice." I was assigned to sing the role of the messenger for the performances.

EIRNS/Stuart Lewis

Gregory Hopkins, accompanied by Sylvia Olden Lee, in Philadelphia, Pennsylvania, July 2, 1993

Several years would pass before I would encounter that dynamo again.

It happened when I entered Curtis Institute of Music. I resented being assigned to the Black coach, but quickly learned that Mrs. Lee was no ordinary instructor.

We established a relationship that went far beyond that of singer and accompanist. Whenever she played for me, she would never allow me to pay her. She would just repeat, "I'm just hanging around until you find someone who can really play for you."

Mrs. Lee always stated that her name stood for "Save Young Lyric Voices In Advance." So, certain repertoire she refused to coach. Once, I was in the finals of a competition for dramatic voices. In a lesson, she darted: "Get someone else to play that; I refuse!" She meant business.

Eventually, I would earn keys to her home. Whenever I came by, she insisted that we work on material. For a moment of relaxation we would play Scrabble, sometimes into the wee hours, after which she would remind me that it was too late for me to drive home, and would insist that I bed down on the other twin bed that was in her bedroom. Mrs. Lee insisted that I always had to be learning something. You will never believe the words I learned while playing Scrabble with her. A true master of vocal repertoire, and a wonderful human being.

No one coaches like Mrs. Lee. Many a time she would command, "Now sing it again, more legato, and make me believe it"—and before I could finish the line, she would yell: "Phoney"!

'Saving Voices, Saving Grace': The Urgent Necessity for C=256

A longtime associate of the Schiller Institute, the recently retired conductor Anthony Morss now serves as a board member of the New York City-based Foundation for the Revival of Classical Culture, which co-sponsored the June 26 Sylvia Lee musical tribute, which he addressed as follows. In 1990, Maestro Morss conducted a concert version of Beethoven's opera "Fidelio" at Lincoln Center's Alice Tully Hall at the C=256 tuning, the first time such a thing had been done in the United States.

Conductor Anthony Morss

Good Afternoon. A lot of us here are old friends; we've been working together for a number of years. But I'm to speak on the topic "Saving Voices, Saving Grace." The tuning problem, which we have solved, in large part, is solved on the basis partly of scientific information, because middle C at 256 [Hertz—i.e. cycles per second] is a major scientific constant, and partly, and I think actually mostly, by demonstrating how much better things sound at the proper pitch. But I'm going to throw you a few crumbs of musicality just to show you how fascinating this subject is.

Bach's Dilemma

In Europe, every city in the Seventeenth and Eighteenth Centuries tuned at a different pitch. And different churches within the same city tuned at a different pitch. Why was this? Partly because a lot of the sacred music depended on the organs, and organs tended to be pitched very high in Europe. People liked the brilliant attack, but nobody wanted to sing up there. So Bach, for example, in Leipzig, had an organ that was tuned a half tone above A=440. He didn't want his chorus and soloists to be singing at that pitch at all. But what to do? He had to transpose it down. So he transposed the organ parts down two semi-tones, that is to say a whole tone down. That means that if the cantata were written in D minor,

the organ part was copied out in C minor, a whole tone lower. And at C minor is where Bach and his singers and his string players of the orchestra would have been pitched. Now, probably Bach would have preferred to tune at 430, because he did have a book by Kepler in his library, and he was familiar with Kepler's ideas. So probably he wanted to do that.

He *couldn't* do that. To tune down an organ in those days was almost as expensive as buying a new one. It doesn't happen to be so today, but it was then. So Bach was stuck. When Handel came to London, London was tuned about a whole tone lower than the current pitch, and went up in 1744 to a half tone lower. In other words, at that point, Handel's orchestra was tuned at the same pitch as Bach's orchestra and organ in Leipzig were pitched. Gradually, the tuning became a little more homogeneous, and around the time of the Viennese classics—Haydn, Mozart, Beethoven, Schubert, Mendelssohn—it was generally accepted that you tuned at about 430. It wasn't universal, but it was a standard and it is very obvious that the great composers of the Nineteenth Century and late Eighteenth Century tailored their musical writing to correspond to the register shifts created by tuning at the proper tuning, namely A=432 or 430.

[Note: The range of tuning for C=256 is A=427-432 cycles per second, a tonal "orbit" rather than a mathematical value as such.]

Variety of Pitches

But to give you an idea of the variety of pitches: Frederick the Great, who was a very good and enthusiastic flute player, and actually even composer of flute concerti, as was his sister, by the way… They were not very good pieces, but the fact that a king should be a competent composer is a bit of a surprise. And he was quite a good player, in spite of, perhaps, a reckless approach once in a while. At the end of one allegro he asked his teacher, Josef Joaquim Quantz, if he liked his tempo, and Quantz replied, "I liked *all* of them, sire." But he was an enthusiastic player and a skilled one. And Quantz not only was his *Kapellmeister* and his music teacher and his flute teacher, but Quantz was also a creator of a flute for Frederick the Great, that came with six different tuning rings. If you don't use any of them you have a seventh possibility of tuning. Why? Because music came from all over, from so many pitches, and to do it justice you had to tune your instrument to that particular pitch, and Frederick's flute had seven possibilities of tuning. That indicated an enormous variety of tuning pitches.

I'll give you one more example from the old times. A friend of mine who was a tenor who sang *Rigoletto* with me many times,— he was a wonderful Duke, which means that he was not only a tenor, but a tenor with a voice with a rather high tessitura, because the Duke was one such. He was such a good performer that he was hired by the Paris opera,— they were doing a revival of an opera by Gluck that had been premiered in the Mid-eighteenth Century and I forget if it was *Iphigenia in Tauris, Iphigenia in Aulis,* one of those. And my friend, the tenor, said it was *impossible.* The part was written so outrageously high—it was a terrible thing to have to sing. He said he didn't know how Gluck could have asked for anything so cruel. Well, *he* didn't know, and *I* didn't know at that point, that when Gluck's opera premiered at the Paris opera in those days, the opera tuned a minor third lower than current pitch. That meant that an aria which on the page which was an F major, in fact sounded a D major. So you can imagine that it was impossible to sing. The principle is very plain. If you live in a city which tunes high, like Venice, which tuned at modern 440—surprisingly enough, the only one that I know of—then you write pitches that are very low, because you are aiming to get all the music in the usable middle range of the voice—that's perfectly obvious—without extraordinary high notes and extraordinary low notes. And, consequently, if you are in a city which tunes very low, you write high notes, higher notes, in order to keep in that same usable middle register of the voice, which everybody wants to sing in. So it shows you can't take literally, by modern pitch standards, any of those old scores.

Saving Modern Voices

I remember years ago I conducted a wonderful Polish violinist named Henry Szeryng; he was a Carl Flesch pupil in Berlin. Mr. Szeryng had recorded one of the concerti we were doing—we were doing the Mozart Seventh and the Tchaikovsky. He had recorded the Tchaikovsky with [the conductor Charles] Munch and the Boston Symphony, so I bought the recording to find out what he was going to do. I was amazed I could follow every twist and turn. Anyway, Mr. Szeryng had just come from the Vienna Philharmonic, and Vienna had been made one of the leaders in high tuning in recent times by Herbert von Karajan, and here we come to the whole business of saving modern voices, because Karajan liked to tune high. Why? Because it made the orchestra brilliant, it gave it a cutting edge. But, unfortunately that's called interference, for the singers. And I once conducted a "Cav/Pag" (*Cavalleria Rusticana/ Pagliacci*) at official French pitch established in 1859-1860 (A=435), and the balance problem of the opening of Pagliacci with the high screaming violins and piccolos and flutes was all resolved perfectly, I didn't have to say anything. Usually I have to balance that passage very well. But anyway, to return to Mr. Szeryng, he said that the high tuning of the Vienna Philharmonic bothered not only his ears, but it bothered his actual finger positions. They were significantly different, and he felt quite uncomfortable playing there.

Now, von Karajan had a habit of tuning both the Berlin Philharmonic, which he controlled, and the Vienna Philharmonic quite high. Well, then, if you're dealing with heroic roles that have an upper limit to the pitches they can hit, you're often tuned out of the use of really heroic voices. So what do you do? You hire lighter voices that may have an extra note in their compass. So they can hit the pitches now, with the orchestra tuned high. But look out! The orchestration hasn't changed, and the orchestration was a heavier orchestration for heavy voices. If the heavy voices just can't hit the pitches, you hire lighter voices. What's wrong with that? Well, the color is all wrong for the role. Even though the conductor may say, don't worry, "I'll keep the orchestra down," sooner or later those heavy accompaniments are going to do real damage to the voices.

And I will never forget an interview I heard with Elisabeth Schwarzkopf—spoke quite good English, by the way—and she said she was so lucky when she began to sing one of her signature roles, Die Marschallin in *Der Rosenkavalier,* and she said, "I was so lucky to have Herbert von Karajan in the pit, because Herbert can make the orchestra go away." But what is that really telling you? That that role was not for her in the first place. You wanted Lotte Lehmann for that role, not Elisabeth Schwarzkopf, who had a greatly artistic method of singing, but whose voice was rather white, and rather thin in contrast to the richness of a Lotte Lehmann.

So, another very close friend of mine, with whom I worked for years and years and conducted her in more performances than I can recall,—she had sung in Europe for some years, and she went back to Europe to sing in Bulgaria, in both Sofia and in Varna, the two biggest cities, and she sang *Aida* and she sang *Tosca*, and she said to her husband, who was a piano technician as well as a tenor, "What's the matter with this orchestra? I'm singing *Aida*, and in the third act I have this rise floating up to the high C which is meant to be sung pianissimo. I can float that easily without any trouble normally. Here I have to yell as loud as I can yell to get the note up,—what's going on?" And her husband said, "My dear, even the pianos in this opera house are tuned to 451." Disaster! So they wanted her to come back and sing Elisabetta in *Don Carlo*, and she said "I'm coming back only of you can get your orchestra down to 440 where it belongs." She wasn't even talking about the ideal pitch of 432 but even down to a normal 440. They couldn't do it.

Solving the Problem

We are now engaged in research to find out what to do to alter the wind instruments. Strings can just tune down to the proper tuning. Winds have much more difficulty in doing that. There is a limit to what they can do. If you push a woodwind instrument all the way to where all the parts are very tight, that's as high as your pitch is going to go. If you pull it out slightly, that's as low as your pitch is going to go. There are limitations. Fortunately we have a member of our organization who is a bassoon player, and he got a slightly larger mouthpiece and he got slightly larger reeds—and now he is perfectly comfortable with that larger mouthpiece and reed playing at 432. That's wonderful. I've discovered the flutes and the trumpets can be altered.

Now we have somebody in the Washington D.C. area who plays horn for us, who has figured out how to get the horns down. When I tried it years ago, the hornists just pushed their hands deeper and deeper into the horn to lower the pitch, and they had to play much louder to be heard, and they ended up with sore lips and they said they would never do it again.

So we have to solve those problems, and we are in the process of solving them, because the actual physical difference of beauty and roundness and the fullness of the sound is unmistakable. Both in the Eighteenth and Nineteenth Centuries there were laboratory experiments with some of the great Italian eighteenth-century stringed instruments to discover at what range they achieved their greatest sonority, their greatest roundness of sound, their greatest resonance, actually. And we know that greatest resonance means greatest roundness and greatest mellowness and greatest beauty of sound. And both experiments in both centuries came up with the same figures. Between 427 and 432 was the optimum resonance for all of these beautiful Italian stringed instruments. This is not a matter of laymen's opinion. This is a matter of scientific determination.

Something Has Gone Seriously Wrong

So, when you have people like von Karajan asking lyric voices like Mirella Freni to sing *Aida,* you know something has gone very seriously wrong with the entire casting process. If the orchestras tune so high that only lighter voices can sing the roles, then you are falsifying the entire character of the music. Because although you have a voice that can hit the notes, it is not of the right color and it is not of the right weight, and it doesn't work with the orchestration, and I can tell you no matter how hard the conductor may try to keep the orchestra down so he doesn't injure the voices, sooner or later light voices singing heavy roles will be severely damaged.

The great Italian conductor Giulio Serafini said at one point, "if they keep up this absurdly high tuning pitch, it will be the end of the Italian lyric theater." Just like that. The end of the opera house if we keep tuning up here at these ridiculous pitches! And I wonder if opera wouldn't be a whole lot more popular today, especially in Eastern Europe, where Vienna is 448 for example or Varna 451—absolutely, totally impossible. Opera, I think would be much more popular if you had the correct tuning and you had voices naturally in the proper respect to pitch.

I would only say that if you notice so many of the opera stars in recent years have come from England or the United States, which is where the pitch is still down at 440 or 442; in Europe, especially in Eastern Europe, the pitch is so high, that very few singers come to the Met now that are not already burnt out. So we have many more English and American opera singers than we do from Italy, which used to be the great fountain of them. Anyway, one could go on forever, but thank you for your indulgence.

III. Russia and China

Russia and China Combine Efforts to Preserve World Peace

by William Jones

July 2—While the Obama Administration is rapidly pushing the world toward nuclear war in Europe and in Asia, the leaders of China and Russia have agreed to redouble their efforts—and their partnership—in order to offer to the world the possibility of a new directionality toward peace and development and away from the present path toward war. Immediately following the summit meeting of the Shanghai Cooperation Organization, which is now in the process of adding India and Pakistan to its membership, and represents around half of the world's population, the meeting in Beijing of the two presidents represents an absolutely ground-breaking development.

kremlin.ru

After the expanded meeting of the SCO Council of Heads of State in Uzbekistan, June 23-24, Russian President Vladimir Putin (center) seen with China President Xi Jinping (on Putin's left) and President of Uzbekistan Islam Karimov (left).

The Joint Declaration issued by the two presidents takes aim at the underlying problem: the role adopted by the United States, during the successive presidencies of George W. Bush and Barack Obama, to act as the "Roman Legion" for the crisis-ridden and collapsing British trans-Atlantic London/Wall Street System, a role which has propelled the United States and the NATO alliance into a desperate drive to assert their will and dominance everywhere in the world. This grave threat has been further enhanced by the mental instability of a Barack Obama who views his own role as maintaining the sadistic geopolitical position of the United States as the world's sole remaining "superpower."

In the Joint Declaration, Russia and China voiced great concern over the increasingly "negative factors" affecting the global strategic stability. "Some countries and military-political alliances seek decisive advantage in military and relevant technology," the statement

reads, "so as to serve their own interests through the use, or threatened use of force in international affairs," the statement says. "Such a policy has resulted in an out-of-control growth of military power and has shaken the global strategic stability system."

A New Type of Relationship

Most significantly, the Joint Declaration characterizes the relationship of their two countries as a "major power relationship," a characterization that China also applies to its relationship with the United States, but which U.S. representatives have refused to utter, as it would tend to diminish its status as a de facto "imperial" power. The joint declaration also lays out the principles undergirding their relationship, principles which should serve as a universal norm for relations between sovereign nations, namely, respect for the other's particular choice of development path, non-interference in

U.S. Department of Defense

The Aegis Ballistic Missile Defense system, an integrated naval weapons system targeting Russia, shown firing a test missile.

Missile Defense Agency

A launch of the THAAD missile defense system in the Asia-Pacific, targeting China.

the internal relations of the other, mutual support in the core questions of sovereignty, defense, development, the principle of win-win all-sided cooperation, and a rejection of confrontation.

"The signing of this agreement and its practical realization will have an important international dimension," the statement says, "demonstrating to the entire world a successful example of the establishment of harmonic, constructive, equal, trustworthy, and mutually beneficial relations between major powers. The agreement between Russian and Chinese strategic foreign policy established on the basis of this cooperation will become a major factor in international life, permitting the formation of a just and rational multipolar world." In the declaration, the two sides also commit themselves to bringing this new model of international relations to the United Nations. "Russia and China base themselves on the fact that the world architecture is experiencing a rapid evolutionary transformation in connection with the ongoing redistribution of forces on the world stage."

Combating Interventionism

"The two parties support the idea of taking a resolution to the UN General Assembly condemning intervention and interference in a country's internal affairs, opposing regime change in any country through unlawful intervention from the outside, and even through the extraterritorial use of the laws of one country in violation of international law." The two sides also condemned the imposition of unilateral sanctions without the backing of a UN mandate.

The Declaration also underlines the growing importance of multilateral institutions such as BRICS and the SCO in the formulation of the norms and procedures in the international arena. The two sides reiterated their unity as victorious allies during the war against fascism and as permanent members of the UN Security Council in upholding the rule of law as this has been defined by the United Nations after the defeat of fascism. The document also throws down the gauntlet to the unilateral interventionism of the United States and Britain during the last few decades which has caused so much chaos in the world. "Some countries and military-political alliances seek decisive advantage in military and relevant technology, so as to serve their own interests through the use, or threat of the use, of force in international affairs. Such a policy has resulted in an out-of-control growth of military power and has shaken the global strategic stability system," the Declaration says.

The Declaration condemns the deployment of missile defense systems, characterizing these as totally destabilizing, particularly the Aegis systems targeting Russia and the THAAD systems in the Asia-Pacific, targeting China. It also condemns the Prompt Global Strike system. "The long distance precision attack weapons developed by some countries, such as the global system for instant attack, may seriously damage the strategic balance and trigger a new round of the arms race," the statement read.

July 8, 2016 **EIR**

Our Mission to Mortality   31

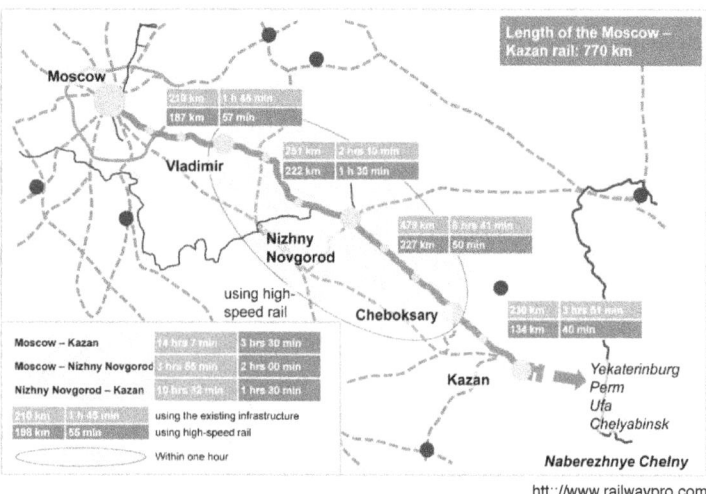

htt://www.railwaypro.com

The Moscow-Kazan rail line is a key element connecting to the Chinese Belt and Road initiative.

Creating Synergy in Economic Development

The thirty agreements signed by the two parties indicate the efforts they have taken to combine China's Belt and Road Initiative with the Russian-backed Eurasian Economic Union. While many of the agreements are follow-ups to the oil and gas deals already concluded, there was also a panoply of other agreements, which are aimed at bringing the Belt and Road and the Eurasian Economic Union into a collaborative relationship. The Joint Declaration underlines the complementarity of the two nations' development

video grab/Russia Beyond the Headlines

Russia-Chinese cooperation to jointly develop rocket engines was one of many agreements reached by President Putin and President Xi in their post-SCO summit meeting in Beijing June 25.

projects, in particular Russia's plans to develop its Far Eastern regions and China's plans to revitalize its former industrial hub in China's northeast. The declaration also noted the complementarity between the development of their two riverine programs, in the Volga region of Russia and in the Yangtze Development Zone in China. In his comments to the press after the meeting with the Chinese President, Putin indicated that over twenty agreements have been signed within this particular format.

The two sides agreed to move forward on financing and construction of the high-speed rail system between Moscow and Kazan, a key element of the Belt and Road Initiative. China will also invest in the Yamal liquid gas project in Russia's Far North. Agreements were signed to increase the export of Russian wheat to China and the

construction of a major grain terminal in the southern Baikal region close to the Chinese border, creating what Putin called a "new land grain corridor." China will also invest in several grain elevators in the region.

Nuclear energy will continue to be a major area of development, with Russia prepared to build two more reactors in China's Tianwan nuclear plant. The two countries will also work together to build a wide-bodied airplane and a new heavy-duty helicopter for both civilian and military use. Cooperation will also continue in aerospace. In their 2013-2017 program of cooperation in space, they will deepen their work on Earth observation, the study of the Moon and the outer planets, and the development of rocket engines, and they will conduct practical work in space navigation through collaboration between the satellite navigation systems of Russia (the GLONASS program) and China (the Beidou system).

Speaking to the press after their meeting on June 25, President Xi stressed the strategic importance of their relationship. "President Putin and I have unanimously decided that the more complicated the international situation, the more determined we should be, guided by the spirit of strategic cooperation and the idea of eternal friendship. We should strengthen mutual support, enhance mutual political and strategic trust and cooperation, and unswervingly deepen our relationship."

The two sides have "almost identical views" on international issues, Putin said, and he underlined the importance of their cooperation in the SCO, the BRICS, and the United Nations. Both Xi and Putin are looking forward to the Sept. 4-5 G20 Summit in Hangzhou, where many of these issues of reforming international governance and avoiding war will no doubt be front and center. Given the escalating world-wide chaos and military dangers that are being spread by British-backed terrorism and the insane interventionism of the Obama Administration, this "new paradigm" is certain to muster strong support from the nations gathered there.

THINK LIKE PUTIN, NOT LIKE McCLELLAN

How to Win the Battle Before Us

by Robert Ingraham

There is a difficulty which arises when the subject of human "genius" enters into a discussion. If one points to Albert Einstein, Alexander Hamilton, Krafft Ehricke, or others as examples of "genius," for many, even among otherwise intelligent and insightful people, the topic under discussion suddenly becomes mysterious, unintelligible. The concept of "genius" takes on an other-worldly character, something beyond human comprehension, a subject not accessible to human deliberation.

Even the mere word "genius" evokes apprehension, panic, or blank incomprehension. People simply say, "I am not a genius, and these other god-like creatures whom you have named, who possess this great talent, are beyond my ability to comprehend. Genius may be fine and good, but I am just a practical person."

This problem has worsened in recent decades, as the issue of creativity and genius has been deliberately obfuscated by the trans-Atlantic oligarchy. This is one of the reasons that rock stars or Silicon Valley digital coders are referred to as "geniuses" in today's popular culture. In art and music, genius has become an utterly irrational concept, often connected to the introduction of something that is simply new, shocking, or different, no matter how degraded or linear in concept.

What has been lost is the true role of genius in transforming human soci-ety, in intervening into human culture in a way that creates new potential "up-shifts" in thinking and unleashes new potencies for changing the directionality of future events. There is enormous power which lies dormant in the hearts and minds of human individuals, power which is located not in monetary greed or simple animal passions, but in the normally unaccessed creative qualities of mind that constitute the true nature of our species, of what it means to be human. This power, this potential, exists—to one degree or another—within the minds and souls of every single human being. Properly nourished, it will emerge. With some, it will become the driving force of their individual identity, for others less so; but all can partake in its ebullience, for it is that creative power which defines the term "human being."

kremlin.ru

The seventh BRICS summit in Ufa, Russia, July 8-9, 2015. From left: Brazil President Dilma Roussef, Indian Prime Minister Narendra Modi, Russian President Vladimir Putin, Chinese President Xi Jinping, and South African President Jacob Zuma.

Russian President Vladimir Putin (center, arm extended) participating in the Shanghai Cooperation Organization Heads of State meeting in Tashkent, Uzbekistan, June 24, 2016, marking its 15th anniversary.

I. The Manichaean Dilemma

There is a certain way in which one might describe the current strategic situation in the world. It goes something like this:

There are two competing tendencies. On the one side is to be found the BRICS, the Shanghai Cooperation Organization, the 'One Belt, One Road' policy, and the nations allied with these efforts for global economic development. On the other side is the trans-Atlantic (British) imperial system, the collapsing London/Wall Street financial system and the military threat of NATO. These two adversaries are now engaged in a struggle for the future direction of human affairs. Humanity is at a fork in the road, faced with two alternative paths.

But is that really the best way to understand our current situation? Even more importantly, how does such an analysis, of an apparent struggle between good and evil, aid us in developing the means to win the fight before us in the weeks ahead?

In posing the issue as one of "war versus economic renaissance," there are two problems. The first is that such a construct does not define a means whereby a victory might be won. The second is that such an approach is not coherent with either how the human mind works, nor how great breakthroughs have occurred in the past. Human history is not a stationary battle between good and evil, but rather the deployment of great "flanking" interventions which redefine the potential power for human advancement, interventions which create new possibilities, previously unimagined. This is true whether the arena is scientific progress, musical composition, a military battlefield, or a political struggle.

Take the case of Filippo Brunelleschi. When Brunelleschi began his work on the dome of the Florence Cathedral (*Cattedrale di Santa Maria del Fiore*) in 1420, Europe was just beginning to recover from the dark age collapse of the 14th Century. Between 1322 and 1363, more than 70% of the population of Europe had died from disease and starvation, and life expectancy had dropped from 35 years to 17 years. European society, finance and culture were dominated by parasitical oli-

Filippo Brunelleschi made the breakthroughs that made possible the completion of the Santa Maria del Fiore cathedral and its dome, in Florence, Italy.

This hoist for lifting building materials was invented by Brunelleschi so the dome could be built, contributing to the successful implementation of Brunelleschi's advances in physical science.

garchical families, centered in Venice and other locations. Illiteracy was the norm for the general population.

In taking on the challenge to construct a dome for the *Santa Maria del Fiore* Cathedral, a task which was considered impossible by the engineers and architects of that era, it fell upon Brunelleschi to do what had never been done before, to build a type of physical structure which had never been built before—a self-sustaining conical octagonal dome, without the use of a wooden infrastructure or outer buttresses. Brunelleschi's design was denounced by almost everyone; he was called a "a buffoon and a babbler." Yet, is was in the solutions that Brunelleschi discovered that we find the origins of modern physical science, and it was in the works of his protégé Paolo Toscanelli and Toscanelli's friend Nicholas of Cusa that this approach to physical science was further developed, leading into Johannes Kepler's examinations into the nature of the solar system.

Cusa's insights into the nature of the human mind and its relationship with physical science are further explored in his *On Learned Ignorance* and *On God as Not-Other*, and it is, in particular, his notion of the "self-moving mind" which points the way towards victory in our current crisis of 2016.

Brunelleschi's willful intervention transformed the potential for a revolutionary development within human society. It created scientific and cultural possibilities which had hitherto not existed, this at a time when the human condition appeared hopeless. Brunelleschi launched the Renaissance.

As Saint Augustine rigorously demonstrated, evil has no real positive existence; it is purely a negative phenomenon. Human creativity, properly understood and vigorously deployed, will always overcome the

Paolo dal Pozzo Toscanelli was a protégé of Brunelleschi.

Cardinal Nicholas of Cusa.

Johannes Kepler.

St. Augustine.

evil (entropic) forces or tendencies within society. It is the only force capable of doing so, for a creative intervention is not a fight *against* something; it is an action which brings into play a more powerful future potential within society. When evil appears to triumph over good, this is almost always because those who are opposing evil have allowed themselves to fight on a battlefield, whose rules and conduct are limited in scope and defined by the enemy.

II. Military Mistakes

General George McClellan has gone down in history books as a commander who suffered from timidity, who was afraid to attack. This characterization, however, does not adequately describe the nature of his failings.

Beginning in March of 1862, McClellan moved an army of 122,000 men to Fort Monroe, Virginia and initiated what became known as the Peninsula Campaign, which would last for five months. The intention was to capture the Confederate capital at Richmond. Despite outnumbering the opposing forces in men, artillery, ships, and supplies during every step of the campaign, McClellan's efforts failed spectacularly.

McClellan was not simply timid. He was obsessed by the imagined power of his enemy. Fear and doubt ate at him. The most extreme example of this was early in the campaign, when he refused to attack Confederate forces holding the city of Yorktown. Instead he ordered a siege, which lasted three weeks. He spent almost all of the time building emplacements for scores of siege guns. He was convinced he was facing an enormous Confederate army, and he wrote to President Lincoln that he was outnumbered two-to-one. In reality, the

President Abraham Lincoln confronting Gen. George McClellan at Antietam, Md. after McClellan refused to pursue Confederate General Lee after Lee's defeat at the Battle of Antietam.

Confederate forces holding Yorktown numbered 13,000, and they were very poorly supplied.

Through May and June, McClellan moved slowly up the Peninsula, fighting inconclusive battles at both Williamsburg and Seven Pines. The Union Army did not win either of those battles, but was able to advance simply because the outnumbered Confederates withdrew towards Richmond each time. By June 1, McClellan was on the outskirts of Richmond, but he again refused to attack Confederate lines, despite still having a two-to-one superiority in numbers.

Throughout these weeks, McClellan wrote feverishly to Lincoln and Secretary of War Stanton, reporting that he was outnumbered, facing a Confederate Army of more than 200,000, when it was actually 55,000. He described non-existent Confederate troop movements and flanking operations, and he warned that his army was in danger of being annihilated.

Then, from June 25 to July 1, the Confederate Army launched a series of very-limited counterattacks, known as the Seven Days Battle. Despite suffering no major defeat, and actually having won several of the battles, McClellan ordered

a general retreat, pulling his army most of the way back down the Peninsula, where they sat, behind defensive positions, until Lincoln ordered their withdrawal in August.

McClellan was obsessed with the enemy, with the power—or imagined power—of the enemy, of what *they* might do, of how *they* might attack. His pre-occupation was in defending his army from attack. It was *set piece* warfare. McClellan's primary failure was that he based all of his actions on what the enemy was doing or what they might do, and he *reacted* to these hostile actions or possible actions.

Compare this with Douglas MacArthur, prior to the 1950 Inchon Landing in Korea. In the councils of war, prior to that amphibious invasion, MacArthur was alone, completely alone, in insisting on his invasion plan. Much like Brunelleschi in 1420, everyone disagreed with him. Later, after the great flanking attack succeeded, MacArthur stated that the moment he knew he was right about his invasion plan, was when everyone else opposed it, that if they all thought it couldn't work, then the North Koreans would think so too and wouldn't defend against it.

For MacArthur, the only consideration was "How do you win?" The only thing worth creating was a *Strategy for Victory*.

General Douglas MacArthur (seated) observing the attack by his forces at the battle of Inchon, Korea, Sept. 15, 1950.

III. Vladimir Putin and Lyndon LaRouche

As this article is being written, Russian President Vladimir Putin has just arrived in Beijing, China for extensive talks with Chinese President Xi Jinping and other Chinese leaders. These meetings follow directly on the heels of the June 23-24 Tashkent summit of the Shanghai Cooperation Organization (SCO), where Putin, Xi, Indian Prime Minister Modi and other Asian leaders met to discuss several pressing issues, including proposals for greatly enhanced collaboration between the SCO and the Eurasian Economic Union (EEU).

These portentous discussions between the leaders of India, Russia, and China occur at a moment when worldwide strategic potentials are developing and changing at a breathtaking pace. Of all these developments, perhaps the most significant has been the continuing intervention that Vladimir Putin, together with Xi Jinping, is making into Europe. This includes Xi's June 17-24 seven-day Silk Road Tour, which included stops in both Serbia and Poland and the staggering breakthrough which took place at the June 16-18 conference of the St. Petersburg International Economic Forum. At that latter event, President Putin, in a way which evoked the historic memory of the "westernizer" Peter the Great, offered full partnership and participation for all of the European nations in the great economic and scientific opportunities which are being opened up by Russia, China, the SCO, the EEU, and the One Belt, One Road policy. The point was made strongly by Putin, in the form of an offer, that the unfolding economic renaissance is intended for all of Eurasia, not simply the Asian nations. European participation in the huge Eurasian projects, involving high-speed rail, nuclear power, and other technologies is not simply an economic program, but an idea, a concept, a potential, which once conveyed to the minds of Europeans, will work its way into all future political actions.

In his remarks to the St. Petersburg Economic Forum, Putin said:

> As early as June we, along with our Chinese colleagues, are planning to start official talks on the formation of comprehensive trade and economic partnership in Eurasia with the participation of the European Union states and China. I expect

Press Information Bureau, Government of India

Indian Prime Minister Narendra Modi and Russian President Vladimir Putin, at the bilateral meeting on the sidelines of the Shanghai Cooperation Organization (SCO) summit in Tashkent, Uzbekistan, June 24, 2016.

> that this will become one of the first steps toward the formation of a major Eurasian partnership...
>
> Friends, the project I have just mentioned—the greater Eurasia project—is, of course, open for Europe, and I am convinced that such cooperation may be mutually beneficial. Despite all of the well known problems in our relations, the European Union remains Russia's key trade and economic partner. It is our next-door neighbor, and we are not indifferent to what is happening in the lives of our neighbors, European countries, and the European economy.

Cracks and fissures in the London-Obama control over continental Europe are spreading and multiplying. How the successful Brexit vote will affect this process is not clear, but as the chaos and uncertainty spread, it is Putin and his allies who are in the driver's seat—and they are offering Europe a way out. The growing number of German and other leaders who have publicly condemned the recent NATO maneuvers on Russia's borders, together with the high level participation of European leaders in the St. Petersburg Forum, are merely indications of a much deeper and seismic reshaping of the political process now unfolding throughout Europe.

Xinhua/Li Gang

The successful launch, June 25, 2016, of China's Long March-7 carrier rocket from Wenchang Satellite Launch Center. It has been designed to be a workhorse for a planned Chinese space station.

laboration between China and Russia on space exploration, an expanding effort which now also includes India and many other countries. This involves not only frontier work in science and technology, but also something much more. It was Krafft Ehricke who posited that once humanity begins to move into the solar system, begins to reach beyond the confines of our planet, that this will be the moment when the true nature of our species will begin to emerge. We will no longer be "earthlings"; rather, our mission, and our identity, will be defined by uncovering and mastering the principles which govern the galaxy.

Don't Make McClellan's Mistake

The continuing danger amidst all of this, is the still-ongoing occupation of the White House by Barack Obama, and the London-Washington push for a war confrontation with Russia. Nothing that is said in this article should be taken to minimize this threat. Obama is a killer and a very weak narcissistic personality. Under pressure, he is capable of anything. Nevertheless! Don't repeat McClellan's mistake. Don't be paralyzed by fear of Obama. Don't simply be "against" Obama, or "against" Hillary Clinton or Donald Trump.

Think, instead, of flanking attacks. Think of ways that will awaken new potentials, potentials both within the strategic sphere and within growing numbers of citizens.

The May 5, 2016 "Pray for Palmyra" concert given by the Mariinsky Symphony Orchestra, from St Petersburg, and led by Valery Gergiev, is just such a flank. The power of this concert was that it evoked the beauty of what human culture might be, of what the fight in Syria was *for*, not simply what it was *against*. In particular, the inclusion of the work by Bach was a pointed reminder to the people of Germany of those qualities which have been great in German history.

Perhaps the most powerful flank capable of orienting nations toward a different future is the growing col-

Manhattan

Lyndon LaRouche's Manhattan Project, properly understood, is an outstanding flank. In one sense the Project was initiated to rebuild Mr. LaRouche's organization in the United States, to return it to its original intent, following the damage which was done after the George Bush imprisonment of Lyndon LaRouche and the aftermath of that imprisonment. Yet, a greater purpose, and a greater power, has been unleashed during the last twenty months. A new, fearlessly creative force has been unleashed within the United States through the combination of classical music choruses in three New York boroughs, the Saturday dialogues with Mr. LaRouche, and the recruitment of many individuals into this process.

The power of this process lies not in numbers, but in the fact that it operates outside and against the controlled cultural and political environment. And it tells people the truth. It pricks people's consciences; it provokes them to think; it refuse to play by the rules of the game; it gives people courage.

People both inside and outside of the United States are afraid of Barack Obama. But, ask yourself, outside of the immediate threat of Obama's nuclear arsenal, is

Manhattan Schiller Institute chorus participating in a musical tribute to Sylvia Olden Lee.

he really all that powerful? Can what he, Wall Street, and London represent, that can withstand the power of Beauty? Can they withstand the power of courageous Creative Intervention, of a properly understood flanking attack?

Putin has broken the trans-Atlantic rigged game. The rats holding us back are scurrying for cover. Why be afraid of them? If you are building a house, and a rat gets in the way, the best thing to do is step on the rat and keep building.

IV. The Genius of Krafft Ehricke

Embrace Krafft Ehricke's Age of Reason: No Limits to Growth

by Kesha Rogers

July 1—Over weekend of June 25-26, the Schiller Institute conducted three conferences simultaneously, in Houston, Texas; Berlin, Germany; and New York City, all of which provided clarity that mankind is now on the verge of bringing forth an Age of Reason, defined by peace and cooperation, and grounded on the economic and scientific development of human society. The proceedings of these conferences, taken as a whole, show that we are truly on the verge of a new paradigm and a renaissance for mankind.

This new paradigm can only be brought about through the emergence of a new approach to economic development that is based not on monetary value, but on the creative identity of the human being and the unlimited potential of mankind that is now becoming the dominant principle among leading nations around the world. This system of economic value—implicit in the actions and words of President Vladimir Putin of Russia, President Xi Jinping of China, and Prime Minister Narendra Modi of India, and many others—puts no limitations on human progress and human creative potential.

This is the new dynamic that is now emerging throughout the world, a dynamic of governments that already represent more than 50 percent of the world's population. It is a notion of economic value which must again shape our great republic, as it did in phases of the 19th Century, but it is an outlook which we have long for-

American statesman and economist Henry C. Carey.

gotten. It reminds me of what the great American statesman and economist Henry Carey wrote at that time, that there are two systems in the world.

One of those systems promotes barbarism, poverty, war, and starvation. The other one promotes the strengthening of human identity and human progress. We see now that the system that has been dominating our society—that paradigm of barbarism associated with the zero-growth policies of a dying empire—is now coming to its end. A new approach to human development is emerging. The British monetarist system is collapsing, but if we act now, we can once and for all put an end to this dying financial system and the British Empire, and bring about a world of cooperation, peaceful progress, and scientific and technological development.

When you think about an outlook that understood the conception of mankind's unlimited potential and progress, an outlook that rejected a zero-growth society, one of the greatest examples of it is the Apollo Program and the vision laid out by President John F. Kennedy. For Kennedy's mission was one of the greatest examples of a thrust for mankind to reach an Age of Reason, to continue what the Renaissance had begun.

Kennedy gave a speech on May 25, 1961 that many people remember and think about from time to time. It was the speech in which he announced that we would land a man on the Moon

U.S. President John F. Kennedy paying tribute to astronaut John H. Glenn, Jr. on Feb. 23, 1962, after the first U.S. manned orbital mission earlier that month.

NASA

and return him safely to Earth. But this is not a speech to simply reminisce about. It is not simply a reminder of the "good old days," of a time that is long gone, that can only be fondly remembered.

You must recognize that Kennedy's vision was embodied in the future; it wasn't something that was just to be done in his own time and then forgotten. Kennedy knew that his vision was not just for one nation, but was for the benefit of all nations. That is why it was such a threat to this zero-growth system, which that sought to keep people impoverished, enslaved, and down.

Kennedy knew that accomplishing the mission of landing a man on the Moon and returning him safely to Earth was not for the benefit of the few. It was going to mobilize the best in the nation in science, industry, technology, and education—that the country would meet the challenge of doing that which it had never done before, of creating something entirely new. The intention was to transform mankind, to bring humankind to new levels of character, understanding, and economic existence.

Ehricke's Vision

It is time for many of you to meet the great mind and the contributions of Krafft Ehricke, a dear friend of Mr. and Mrs. LaRouche. He would already be a dear friend

of yours and of all the world, but for the fact that his works have been isolated and in many cases deliberately made unavailable, because of his optimistic view of the creative power and unlimited potential of mankind. Ehricke was not only a brilliant aeronautical engineer and one of the great contributors to the U.S. space program from among the German scientists brought to the United States after World War II: Without Ehricke's vision, a vision which inspired John F. Kennedy, that Moon landing and the return of the voyagers safely to Earth would not have been possible.

Ehricke had the vision of an open world system, that mankind's *extraterrestrial imperative* was to transform cislunar space, the Moon, and other planetary bodies. But that vision could only come about by rejecting the limitations of a zero-growth system, a system that said that mankind is restricted to a single planet of limited resources that we have to continue to fight over.

The Battle Is Joined

Ehricke gave an inspiring speech on the fifth anniversary of that first landing of our species on the Moon on July 20, 1969. In this 1974 speech, Ehricke expressed everything that he was dedicating his life to: He captured the essence of mankind's destiny and the open world of space exploration and colonization. Moving into space, as he correctly understood it, is mankind's extraterrestrial imperative. When you think about that, it's not just a catchy slogan to tickle all the space buffs and gurus. The extraterrestrial imperative is a necessary expression of mankind's unlimited potential. By asserting humankind's extraterrestrial imperative, Ehricke came forward on the battlefield of principle, in a philosophical battle over the truth of mankind's unlimited potential.

It was this battle that Ehricke was waging while the space program—just as it is today—was under brutal attack. When Ehricke was putting forth his extraterrestrial imperative and describing the consequences of an open versus a closed world system, he realized that the dominant policy—and indeed the dominant paradigm—in force at the time was one that demanded limitations on mankind's progress, the paradigm of a system that thought of the spread of the human species as nothing more than the multiplication of mindless waterlilies in a pond. That is what Ehricke took on. That is the paradigm and the system that he waged war against.

At the time of the Apollo missions, there was a major battle going on to reverse the thrust that the Apollo Program represented. The "limits to growth" environmental agenda emerged at this time. And so did policies for financial warfare against the space program and everything that it represented.

It was this for which Ehricke was attacked—his belief in human progress and the unlimited potential of mankind, as expressed also in his engagement with Lyndon LaRouche. It was said that he promoted too much optimism. He had a different view of mankind which he understood to be the only conception that could bring about an Age of Reason. Ehricke was a brilliant mind, and his most fundamental challenge to people was that you cannot put a limit on your human identity. He believed that the right concept of mankind was expressed, and found its rightful place in the Apollo Program, that this represented a new opening and breakthrough for what we are capable of accomplishing.

That is why he said that the Moon landing in July 1969 carried with it the everlasting message that we came in peace for all mankind. Krafft's description of the heritage of Apollo spoke not merely of a cherished past event, but of a future which had not yet been created, a future that could only be brought about by rejecting the dogma of limitations to mankind's potential and progress as found, for example, in the "limits to growth" mobilization.

To Crush American Optimism

Ehricke saw the space program as an opening toward a new Renaissance. The space program was expressing the potential of the human mind and the moral law within mankind that would enable him to open the Age of Reason. He laid out "The Anthropology of Astronautics" in an article with that title in the journal *As-*

NASA

U.S. astronaut salutes U.S. flag July 21, 1969 during the first moon landing, Apollo 11.

tronautics in 1957, which expressed the principles that the space program really represents. But not just the space program. They are the principles by which mankind should live. He stressed three fundamental laws:

1. Nobody and nothing under the natural laws of the Universe impose any limitations on man except man himself.
2. Not only the Earth, but the entire Solar System, and as much of the Universe as he can reach under the laws of nature, are man's rightful field of activity.
3. By expanding through the Universe, man fulfills his destiny as an element of life, endowed with the power of reason and the wisdom of the moral law within himself.

Now that is a person who really lives in the future, and who knows that mankind has a destiny not confined to one small planet! Krafft puts forth this destiny in "The Heritage of Apollo" (1974), in which he gets your imagination going and enables you to understand what we have to do—what our destiny is in exploring and actually transforming our Galaxy. He says—and people just don't think this way anymore:

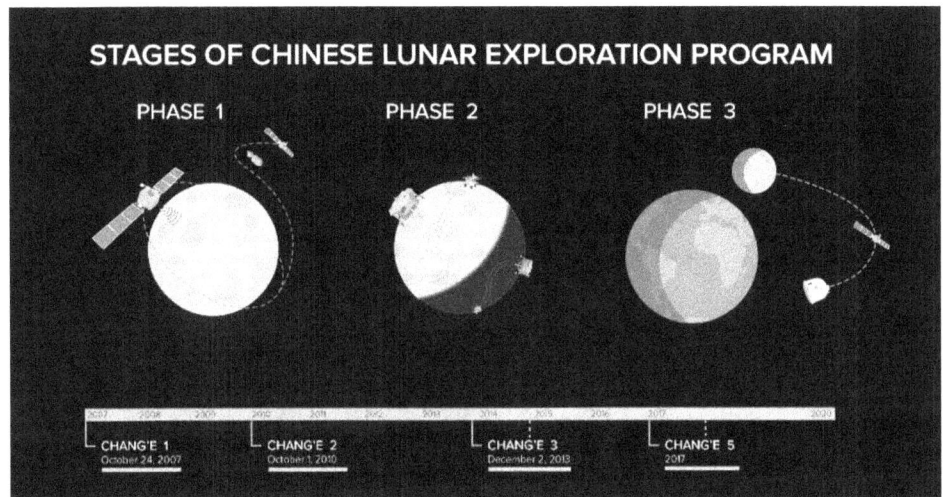

STAGES OF CHINESE LUNAR EXPLORATION PROGRAM

PHASE 1   PHASE 2   PHASE 3

CHANG'E 1
October 24, 2007

CHANG'E 2
October 1, 2010

CHANG'E 3
December 2, 2013

CHANG'E 5
2017

Three stages of the Chinese lunar exploration program. Phase three is slated to be on the back side of the Moon not visible from Earth.

Earth is not an isolated space ship, but travels in the convoy of our star—a luxurious passenger liner flowing through galactic space along with a giant power station and many freighters. Let us not tear up the stateroom furniture to use it for resources. We can board the freighters. It was done on July 20, 1969! The human dimension of Apollo's heritage is a message of hope and confidence, of growth and fulfillment of the human potential. In brief, of a greater and potentially better world, if we make it so.

That optimistic view of man's destiny was one not then shared—and it continues not to be shared—by those who continue to push an anti-science, limits to growth, neo-Malthusian view of man, that we are confined to one small planet, fighting over limited resources. This view exists today. It is what we're up against right now. The targeting of the space program has been rooted in this promotion of pessimism and cultural degeneracy. When we examine the criminal targeting of our space program in the United States, under the atro-

The April 28, 2015 launch of Russia's Soyuz-2.1a from Vostochny Cosmodrome.

kremlin.ru

cious cuts and attacks by President Obama, including the attacks on the manned space program, most people want to see this as matter of money and monetary value. They repeat what they've heard, that there's not enough money, and so we have to take these cuts. But cost is not the real issue; in fact, the space program itself is not the real target.

The target is the optimism of the American people. The objective is to induce Americans to reject their human identity and accept bestialization. Bestialization is what you get when you have a society in which optimism—which enables us to understand that we can accomplish *anything*—is completely taken away. And that is what the scientific community must also come to understand, that this is a war for the minds and the souls of humankind. It is a war for human progress, which is absolutely necessary to lift the people of the United States and the world out of demoralization and despair.

This explains why our space program has been destroyed. It's not a matter of, "Did you agree with this policy?" "Was this policy any good?" The question is, what is society's real intention rooted in, right at this moment? Ehricke attacks the zero-growth outlook that has been the basis for targeting our space program. He explains what limitless growth means by contrasting the concept of the mere multiplication of mankind like lilies in a pond with "the increase in knowledge, in wisdom, in the capacity to grow in new ways." That is what you are seeing emerge right now in the Asia-Pacific region, in China—which has lifted more than 600 million people from poverty. This process is uplifting the world. What are we doing here in the United States? What has happened to us?

The point is, you can't have a Renaissance in a degenerate, dead culture, and you can't have a space program which promotes the true principle of human creativity in a zero-growth society.

People in high places have waged war against the space program, opposing its true intentions. They have made very destructive claims that the space program promotes false optimism, that it promotes the idea that good can come from scientific progress. They say that good will never come from scientific progress! Somebody is going to use it for ill, they say, so it should only be used for the benefit of a very few. All of you who have read Bertrand Russell will hear the echo. He's an evil guy!

This is a false conception of human nature and a dismissal—out of hand—of the idea that a higher and more human culture, one that fosters genius, creativity, and greatly improved conditions of human life for all, could ever exist! Yet this is exactly the kind of orientation to the future that we see in the commitment to peace, human progress, and cooperation now being fostered by such nations as Russia and China.

Fight for *This!*

Ehricke understood that mankind's actions have consequences. He developed a diagram to contrast the consequences of a growing world with those of a no-growth world, as part of his demonstration of the extraterrestrial imperative. **Figure 1** presents half of this diagram, the half that shows the growth paradigm, which he calls the open world system. But to get there, we must also have an understanding of what ideas we have to reject, ideas that have been imposed on mankind to inhibit the progress of science and technology and divert our minds from a renaissance that truly rejects all limitations. If you look at what Ehricke poses here, this is the conception of mankind that we have to be fighting for. This idea of growth is what we see becoming a

FIGURE 1

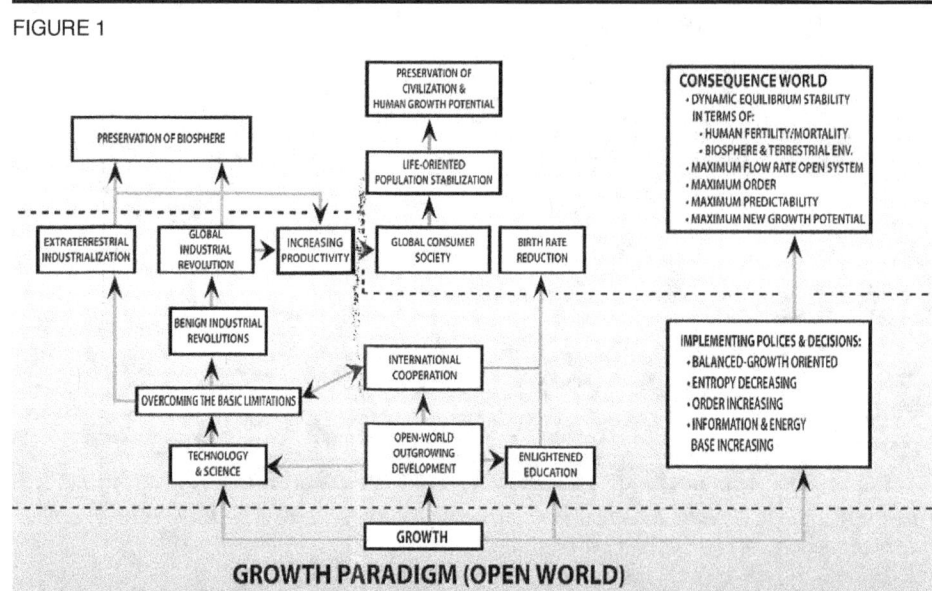

Krafft Ehricke's chart showing the growth paradigm under conditions of no limits to growth, which is a necessary precondition for mankind to carry out its extraterrestrial imperative.

dominant factor in the new paradigm in the world right now.

This view of an open world system that poses no limitations on human progress, was very beautifully expressed, and expressed most emphatically, in a speech by Italian Prime Minister Matteo Renzi in St. Petersburg, Russia last month. He joined others on the podium at the St. Petersburg International Economic Forum and spoke of the need for peaceful cooperation, collaboration, and advances in science and technology that can increase the productivity of mankind. Renzi also talked about increasing the life expectancy of human beings around the planet to 100 years. A hundred years! We used to have some of that. My great grandfather lived to be 103, but he had a strong work ethic and sense of mission in this world. And the food was better then.

But that's the very thing that Prime Minister Renzi was talking about: How to increase life expectancy on the planet through scientific breakthroughs that eliminate disease, poverty, and war, and by achieving the peaceful, beautiful cooperation of mankind. We can bring this about.

You are seeing strong movement in the direction of this new paradigm with the new commion in space exploration, promoting peace among nations. Many international agreements have been signed, including with Russia and China—agreements for cooperation in space that we in the United States should be a part of. We should be collaborating with China as it prepares to

Russian President Vladimir Putin and Prime Minister of Italy Matteo Renzi carrying out a joint press conference on June 17, 2016, during the June 16-18 St. Petersburg International Economic Forum.

accomplish something never done before—going to the far side of the Moon, exploring the far side for the first time, and setting up a facility for radio astronomy in the radio-quiet of the far side, never before exploited. With this cooperation, Ehricke's "poly-global world," looking beyond this Earth, is truly being brought into existence, and the zero-growth paradigm is not going to have any place in our world any longer.

Ehricke's conceptions transform all practical thinking and remove all of the imaginary limitations put on mankind's creative progress. His conceptions go against "living for the moment"— for one's own personal gratification. Ehricke said you come to understand that "Earth and world are no longer synonymous. We no longer live in a closed world of one planet inside a womb of a biosphere. Our world is no more closed than it is flat." Now that's very important, because some of us out there are promoting the idea that we have a flat Earth—the Flat Earth Society. They missed the boat; I don't know where they've been. Ehricke said, "Our world is open to space, and its resources are potentially limitless." It is the human mind which will unlock those unlimited resources of our Universe.

Ehricke had quite an imagination, and he knew that the potential for human progress would transcend and transform mankind's wildest imagination. An artistic depiction of a city on the Moon, done by Ehricke, is shown in **Figure 2**. You can see a museum of astronauts and an indoor rail system—probably a high-speed rail system—all nuclear powered. There are no solar panels. Ehricke saw the Moon as our "seventh continent," where mankind begins to transcend the limitations of physical space.

There are no borders here. There is no war. There is no unipolar dominance; nations and people are living together in harmony. We have to bring this idea forward once again. This is the embodiment of the Age of Reason. This is what the BRICS association of nations is bringing into being right now.

FIGURE 2

Selenopolis, a city on the Moon, as envisioned by Krafft Ehricke. At left is the Hall of Astronauts museum. Note the indoor monorail for getting around in the city. Ehricke's concept of the Moon was as Earth's 'seventh continent.'

‘WE ARE COSMIC CREATURES’

Krafft Ehricke and the Growth of the Noösphere

by Megan Beets

Adapted from a presentation given in Houston on June 25, 2016.

Human reason is a cosmic force. This was expressed as a scientific observation in 1925 by the bio-geo-chemist V.I. Vernadsky in the opening to a paper titled "Human Autotrophy":[1]

There exists now on the terrestrial surface, a great geological force; perhaps cosmic....

This force does not seem to be a new manifestation or special form of energy, nor yet a pure and simple expression of known energy. But it exerts a profound and powerful influence on the course of energetic phenomena on the Earth's surface, and consequently has repercussions—smaller but undeniable—beyond the surface, on the existence of the planet itself.

This force is human reason, the directed and controlled will of social man.

The earliest modern expression of the coherence of human reason with the Cosmos comes from the work of Johannes Kepler (1571-1630). From the moment of the validation of Kepler's discoveries, the Solar system was no longer a distant expanse, out of man's reach, but was an object of *reason*; recreated, recast, as something coherent with the powers of the human mind.

In putting forward his hypothesis that the planets are not merely a collection of lights strewn across the celes-tial sphere whose movements can be observed, measured, and predicted by a model, but rather are moved by a knowable physical cause—a physical power based in the body of the Sun—Kepler created a new science, *astrophysics*, and transformed mankind's relationship to the Solar system.

He further perfected that discovery by demonstrating that the Solar system is not a disorganized collection of bodies which happen to inhabit the same region of space; but while it is not a fixed system, it is a *coherent* system—each planet being "tuned" in its motions to every other, in the same way the coherence of a polyphonic musical composition is brought about when many voices come together in concert to express a single idea.[2]

And so, in the early 17th Century, the Solar system became—in potential—a part of man's domain on which he could act.

However, humanity had to wait nearly 300 years before that potential could be actualized. It wasn't until the early 20th Century, with advancements in our mastery of principles of chemistry and materials science, and the development of powered flight, that space travel came to be something within reach.

Around this time, rocket clubs and societies sprang into existence, as across Germany, the United States, and Russia. The members of these amateur organizations were primarily young men, many of them inspired by the 1929 German film, *Frau im Mond* (*The Woman*

---

1. https://www.21stcenturysciencetech.com/Articles_2013/Fall-Winter_2013/Human_Autotrophy.pdf

2. For more see science.larouchepac.com/kepler/harmony and https://www.youtube.com/watch?v=yV-KcB-nc_E

in the Moon),[3] who experimented with and developed technologies for rockets, rocket propulsion, and flight. The great visionary who would later be a foundation of the U.S. space program, Krafft Ehricke, was part of this exuberant expression of enthusiasm and optimism.

Thought Transforms the Cosmos

Coincident with mankind's first steps toward spaceflight was the life and work of Vladimir Vernadsky. In 1926, Vernadsky published a work for which he is well known, *The Biosphere*.[4] The first section of this great work, "The Biosphere in the Cosmic Medium," begins,

> The face of the Earth viewed from celestial space presents a unique appearance, different from all other heavenly bodies. The surface which separates the planet from the cosmic medium is *the biosphere...*

Vladimir Vernadsky, 1863-1945

Keep in mind that it would be decades before anyone actually did see the face of the Earth from space, but already Vernadsky looked inward upon the Earth from its context in the Cosmos.

He continues,

> A new character is imparted to the planet by this powerful cosmic force.[5] The radiations that pour upon the Earth cause the biosphere to take on properties unknown to lifeless planetary surfaces, and thus transform the face of the Earth. Activated by radiation, the matter of the biosphere collects and redistributes solar energy, and converts it ultimately into free energy capable of doing work on Earth.
>
> The outer layer of the Earth must, therefore, not be considered as a region of matter alone, but also a region of energy and a source of transformation of the planet. *To a great extent, exogenous cosmic forces shape the face of the Earth*, and as a result, the biosphere differs historically from other parts of the planet. This biosphere plays an extraordinary planetary role.[6]

With this thesis stated at the opening, *The Biosphere* is a rigorous documentation and elaboration of the powerful and extraterrestrial nature of life on Earth. Vernadsky, in the tradition of Kepler, abolishes the separation between life and the cosmos.

During the same period, Vernadsky was also considering the unique action of *human* life on the planet. He notes that while non-human life transforms the face of the planet via its metabolism—its nutrition and respiration—creating new chemical combinations and minerals via its body, and depositing these new minerals to shape the geochemistry of the planet, man's biology has not significantly changed for tens of thousands of years, if not longer.[7] However, over that time period, man-

---

3. Fritz Lang's *Frau im Mond* inspired many of Germany's space pioneers, then children or young men, with the idea that humans could use rockets to travel to and explore space. The key advisor to the film was the space visionary, and mentor of many later rocket scientists, Hermann Oberth, a teacher who spent much of his life developing the early ideas and technological concepts to make rocket flight and man's operation in space possible.

4. Vernadsky, V.I. *The Biosphere*. trans. D. B. Langmuir. Springer Science & Business Media, 2012.

5. Here Vernadsky is referring to the radiation, primarily solar radiation, which reaches the Earth from space.

6. Emphasis added.

7. In a 1938 work called "Scientific Thought as a Planetary Phenomenon," Vernadsky makes a rather amusing point, a jab at certain anthropologists, that the cranium of the human skull has been roughly the same size and structure for tens of thousands of years. So, it ain't the size of your brain that matters.

kind's effect on the planet has changed tremendously—in an unprecedented way.

Compare both the quantity and the quality of materials that we as a species create and interact with, and how that has changed over the past 1,000 years—or even the past few decades! Compare where mankind is able to live today and *how* he lives, versus several centuries ago. When you look at man, he has transformed himself as a species so profoundly as a result of the power of reason, that in the beginning of the 20th Century, as Vernadsky notes, the rate at which mankind is transforming the planet—due to the increase in the power of his scientific thought and activity—is beginning to overtake that of the biosphere, despite the fact that the biosphere has also been increasing its effect on the planet over evolutionary time.

The state of the planet where man's reason is the predominant factor of development Vernadsky called the noösphere. This led him to pose a question, included in a short work from 1945:

Here a new riddle has arisen before us. Thought is not a form of energy. How then can it change material processes?[8]

Krafft Ehricke's View of Man in the Cosmos

Krafft Ehricke's own thinking and work was very much shaped by similar considerations. In a 1977 interview, Ehricke recalled his reaction to *Frau im Mond*, when he first considered that human life could evolve off of the planet. "It impressed me enormously. I was at that time twelve years old, and it shocked me into the awareness, all of a sudden: You might be able to leave this planet, to open a new world! And since my interest already at that time was in history and astronomy and the evolution of man, in a very simple way, it kind of gave me a tremendous impulse to interest myself in space. And after two or three years in reading books, and so forth, I became firmly determined that this is an area of technology I wanted to devote my life to."

In his later writings, Ehricke uses the "oxygen catastrophe" of the evolution of life to make a point about human society. Once life reached beyond the Earth for its sustenance, through the development of photosynthesis, taking nourishment from the light of the Sun, the oxygen produced by photosynthesis accumulated in the atmosphere. Oxygen, a highly reactive substance, was toxic to life, and its buildup was poisoning the ecology of the planet. But life developed a new technology: oxygen metabolism, whereby that waste product became a resource.

In a 1974 speech, "The Heritage of Apollo," Ehricke says of life's solution to the "oxygen catastrophe": "Oxygen … no longer was a waste product, but stimulated the evolution of animals, the creation of a stable biosphere through expansion into all regimes of the terrestrial environment, the development of sensors and the brain, and finally the emergence of the human life-form."

Turning to mankind, Ehricke recognized that man, as an element of reason, is inherently not subject to any limitations which tie him to Earth, and is therefore, naturally, also an element of the cosmos. By reaching for the cosmos through his aspirations for rocket flight, mankind was doing that which was necessary, and completely natural.

Ehricke says:

We are cosmic creatures by substance, by the energy on which we operate, and by the restless mind that ceaselessly metabolizes information from the infinitesimal to the infinite; and, on the infrastructure of knowledge, pursues its moral and social aspirations for a larger and better world against many odds. Through intelligences like ourselves, the universe, and we in it, move into the focus of self-recognition. Metal ore is turned into information-processing computers, satellites, and deep-space probes; and atoms are fused as in stars. I cannot imagine a more foreboding, apocalyptic vision of the future than a mankind endowed with cosmic powers but condemned to solitary confinement on one small planet.

Realizing an Extraterrestrial Imperative

But how to begin actualizing mankind's destiny as a cosmic species? Ehricke realized that man does not become a space-faring species by simply hopping on a rocket and zooming through the void of empty space, or by merely setting foot on an alien planet; it is quite the opposite. Man does not move out into empty space; man brings extraterrestrial space—beginning with the Moon and cislunar space—into his domain, into the

---

8. "Some Words About the Noösphere," http://www.21stcenturysciencetech.com/translations/The_Noosphere.pdf

Chris Sloan

An artist's rendition of a Moon colony based on Ehricke's idea of "Selenopolis."

noösphere. Under the influence of human reason, mankind must transform extraterrestrial space into an expanse suitable for man's life and work. In doing this, not only does he begin to transform extraterrestrial space by our action, but in turn, mankind is itself transformed in ways which cannot be fully predicted or anticipated.

Ehricke spent the latter decades of his life concentrating on proposals for a policy of extending the noösphere (though he never used that term) into cislunar and lunar space. At the time of his death in 1984, he was still at work on a program for lunar industrialization, and a posthumously published paper called, "Lunar Industrialization & Settlement: The Birth of Polyglobal Civilization"[9] details some of his proposals.

In that paper, Ehricke puts forward this idea about the Moon:

> It is a seventh continent, almost as large as the Americas. It is large enough to support a civilization. It alone offers the opportunity to create a strong exo-industrial economy, based on highly advanced nuclear, cybernetic, and material processing technologies, ultimately turning large parts of the once-barren lunar surface into a lush

oasis of life, capable eventually of exporting even foodstuffs to orbiting installations, if not to Earth.

Under the section "Lunar Development Strategy," Ehricke states that, "Lunar industry should be viewed as an organism that, over time, evolves to progressively more complex capabilities, and generates sufficiently strong foundations for expansion. Lunar industry must be broad-based and diverse if it is to last. The need for economic feasibility and early returns will require a skillful interplay between market/customer-oriented products and services, and infrastructural investments such as transportation, energy, and surface/space installations that expand food production and diversify industrial productivity."

After enumerating several guiding principles of a development strategy, Ehricke writes, "These principles... are designed to ensure steady progress; early economic viability through ongoing productivity; and supply crisis resistance. (The latter ensures that lunar personnel do not have to return to Earth because they cannot sustain their lunar existence without basic inputs from Earth.)"

This is a long-term perspective, based on moving the noösphere and man's self-sufficiency and power of development out from the planet and onto the lunar surface. To accomplish that, he lays out five stages of development, the final stage of which is the establishment of Selenopolis.[10]

Krafft describes Selenopolis thus:

> [It is a] city-state of lunar civilization...[with a] network of enclosures, gradually expanding to cover many square miles of surface and subsurface... It embodies urban, rural, agricultural, industrial, and resort areas... Selenopolis and the selenosphere are a fully developed lunar world with a large population underwritten by indus-

---

9. http://www.lpi.usra.edu/publications/books/lunar_bases/LSBchapter12.pdf

10. Selene was the ancient Greek goddess of the Moon.

try. This stage [of development] is contingent upon a strong economic foundation, a very high degree of self sufficiency, particularly in food production, and a powerful fusion energy base.

Because, as Ehricke envisions, lunar civilization must largely be economically self-determined, he poses a challenging question:

"Will this be a colony of Earth, part of the common heritage of terrestrial mankind? Or will it be an independent political entity, with Selenians in control of their own world? On a foundation of fusion power, the vast potential of the lunar economy renders the latter alternative possible and hence likely."

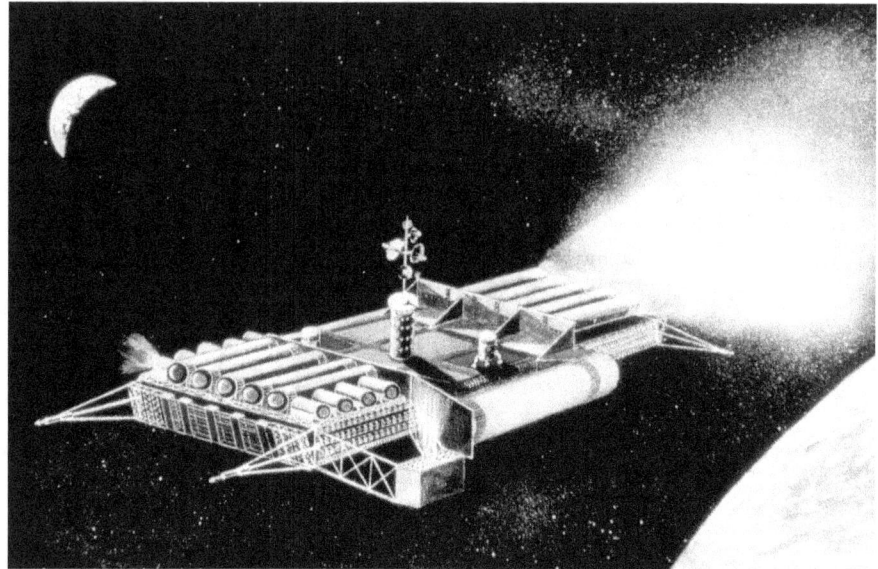

Ehricke's painting shows a nuclear-powered lunar freighter, which uses materials on the Moon for fuel. This is to be part of the transportation infrastructure that will open the Solar System to mankind.

The establishment of such a lunar city-state doesn't come out of nowhere. The development of capabilities, divided among prior development stages, is necessary for the possibility of establishing Selenopolis. One crucial capability is the development of the full utilization of lunar resources. This ranges from the first development stage, which is simply the prospecting and discovery of what minerals are available on the lunar surface, to the establishment of automated mining facilities, which can be attended to by people living in lunar orbit. He calls for the early establishment of production centers for oxygen, necessary both for life-support systems and also for rocket propulsion.

The most advanced stage of development of lunar resources is the establishment of a Central Lunar Processing Complex (CLPC). The CLPC will be a processing center for raw materials, among them aluminum, silicon, iron, glass; intermediate materials such as silicon chips, solar panels, powered metals; and eventually finished products such as machinery, habitats, and so on. It will be supported by remote feeder stations, which will mine resources across the lunar surface and ship the raw materials directly to the CLPC. This will be done either via electric rail, or by a technology first proposed by Ehricke: taking advantage of the low-gravity environment and lack of atmosphere on the Moon, cargo deliveries could be catapulted on a ballistic trajectory to receiver craters.

Another prerequisite for lunar settlement is the securing of an abundant and reliable source of power. Ehricke, among others, concluded that the lunar power source must be nuclear fusion, for two primary reasons. The first is that the lunar night lasts for two weeks, so solar power is out of the question. Even more to the point are the high energy requirements for fuel, materials, and other resource processing, which cannot be met by lower-power regimes. He also implies in this paper, and in other places, that for a number of reasons commercial fusion might be more easily achieved on the Moon than on Earth.[11]

Another prerequisite is that of transportation. Extending man's presence from the Earth to the Moon requires establishing a network of transportation infrastructure. The initial stage called for by Ehricke is to use existing rocket and vehicle technology to create a fleet of ships to ferry the components necessary for a Circumlunar Space Station (CSS) and other communications infrastructure into lunar orbit, and to begin the assembly.[12] The CSS will be a laboratory, a habitat for scientists and engineers, a place of leisure, and a work space. Scientists will be able to descend to the lunar

---

11. Also see Ehricke's 1978 "The Extraterrestrial Imperative." http://www.au.af.mil/au/afri/aspj/airchronicles/aureview/1978/jan-feb/ehricke.html

12. Since Ehricke's time, the United States and other nations have had success at in-orbit assembly and maintenance, as seen in the International Space Station.

surface via a Moon Ferry for exploration and work. He also calls for the development of a fleet of geo-lunar freighters which could make regular deliveries of raw materials, products, and other cargo between Earth orbit and lunar orbit. Many fueling stations are to be positioned between the Earth and the Moon in cislunar space, such that most of the fuel needed to travel between the Earth and Moon would not have to be lifted from the Earth's surface, but could be obtained once in orbit. This is a concept still being discussed today.

Thoughts for the Future

These examples from Ehricke's vision are offered not because his program is exactly what we will implement in every detail, when we finally begin to industrialize the Moon (though, this author suspects, we will find many of Ehricke's proposals to be ahead of their time). They are offered because they are born of a mind committed to thinking of mankind's future as one of limitless growth. His vision is based on a rigorous and scientific understanding of principles of negentropic growth, as also seen in the work of Vladimir Vernadsky. It represents a way of thinking steeped in the same understanding of the nature of the human mind seen in Johannes Kepler.

This is what we must be committed to in a revival of the U.S. space program. Specific proposals aside, the commitment to the limitless progress of man, and nothing less, is primary.

In conclusion, reflect for a moment on Krafft Ehricke, and the great optimism for mankind that he projected. He lived through a very difficult time, in Germany during World War II under the Nazis, through a very uncertain future in the United States, and then had to fight against the environmentalist and other zero-growth attacks on the space program. Through it all, he had a complete optimism for mankind, and he saw man not as a being which fills space; but rather a necessary and beautiful part of the development of the Universe.

As we in the United States move, hopefully, to join the New Paradigm being offered by the nations of Eurasia, we should remember that Krafft Ehricke was born a German, but he was also an American. This is our heritage; it is something we have a responsibility to offer the rest of the world as we move forward into collaboration with China, Russia, and all other nations, with a firm commitment to mankind's unlimited progress.